Bob the Robin & Friends

# Bob the Robin & Friends

## A Love Letter to British Garden Birds

Tony Putman

Gaia

First published in Great Britain in 2026 by Gaia, an imprint of
Octopus Publishing Group Ltd
Carmelite House
50 Victoria Embankment
London EC4Y 0DZ
www.octopusbooks.co.uk

An Hachette UK Company
www.hachette.co.uk

The authorized representative in the EEA is Hachette Ireland,
8 Castlecourt Centre, Dublin 15, D15 XTP3, Ireland (email: info@hbgi.ie)



Distributed in the US by Hachette Book Group
1290 Avenue of the Americas, 4th and 5th Floors
New York, NY 10104

Distributed in Canada by Canadian Manda Group
664 Annette St., Toronto, Ontario, Canada, M6S 2C8



ISBN: 9781856756051
eISBN: 9781856756068

A CIP catalogue record for this book is available from the British Library.

Typeset in 12.5/22pt Loretta by Six Red Marbles UK, Thetford, Norfolk

Printed and bound in Great Britain

10 9 8 7 6 5 4 3 2 1

This FSC® label means that materials used for the product have been responsibly sourced.

FSC
www.fsc.org
MIX
Paper | Supporting responsible forestry
FSC® C104740

To Bob, Bobette, all the robins, animals
and of course our followers

# Contents

# Prologue

I knew Bob the Robin for nearly three and a half years, and in that time I saw him almost daily. During my workday, he'd follow me around the garden where I worked, and on my days off I'd stop by to check how he was doing. We went through highs and lows together over those years and built a strong bond of trust and friendship. But Bob wasn't just my friend: he was adored by thousands from all over the world who followed his daily antics on my social media pages. Many would tune in every single day to see what he was up to. Bob gave me a great insight into the world of robins. He readily allowed me to film his everyday life, whether he was singing from the branch of his plum tree or showing me his beak full of critters as he worked tirelessly to feed his young, as well as his quieter moments, when he simply stood in front of the camera as he happily spent time with me. It was as if he knew that everyone was watching, and he seemed to smile at the world just as it smiled back at him.

When Bob left, the prospect of life without him wasn't just heavy on my heart, it was upsetting for all our followers, too. But the hardest thing of all was the not knowing. We never found out what had happened to him, and there was always a glimmer of hope that he might return. Hope is a powerful emotion, and that was what we all held on to.

My dear friend Bob the robin may have gone, but life in the garden continued. The grass kept growing, the plants still flowered, the birds went on singing and the bees carried on buzzing. There may have been a huge void in my life, but the world did not stop turning, and nor should it have. The garden was a reminder to me that life goes on, and its resilience through every season pushed me to keep going too.

But there were so many memories in the garden that took my mind back to Bob. And, of course, I worried about him. Had something unfortunate happened or did he just find a new partner and move territory? Was he over the hedge – not far away but too far to come home? I didn't know.

The successors to Bob's territory were two younger robins, Bobbin and Bobette. They were a great distraction, and gave me something positive to focus on. They could never be a replacement for Bob, but they were new personalities to get to know and understand. Though in the back of my mind I clung onto the hope that maybe, just maybe, Bob might one day come home, I also didn't mind making new friends along the way, and I was excited for what another year of life in the garden might bring.

# Chapter One

# Life with Bob

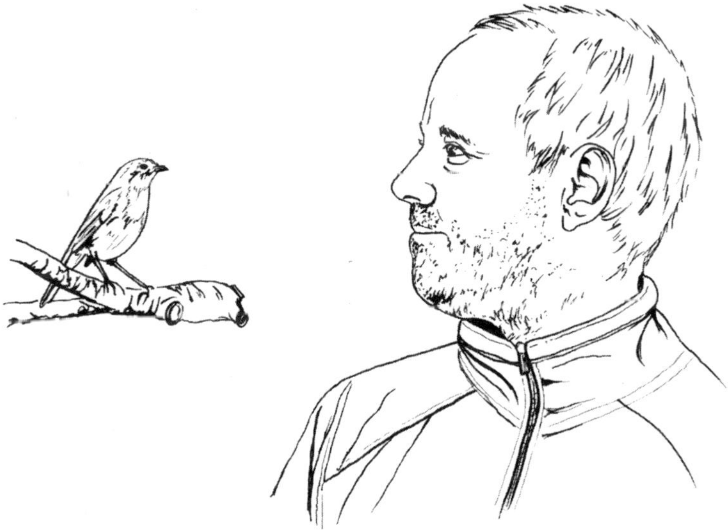

My home town of Edenbridge sits in a valley in the south-east of England, having been built up along the Roman road that led from London all the way to Lewes in Sussex. I've always had a deep and nostalgic love for the town and have always valued its historical heritage. I would often walk the high street trying to imagine the past and what it looked like, knowing that some of the buildings that date back centuries had seen thousands of faces come and go, with mine a small addition to that long line before me. In years gone by there would have been Romans marching north or south along the straight road, or members of the House of Tudor making their way to the south coast or to Starborough Castle, a couple of miles south-west of the town.

Henry VIII, one of Britain's most famous kings, may have been spotted here, perhaps on a hunting trip to Knole Park near his lodging at

Penshurst Place, or visiting Hever Castle just two miles away, the childhood home of his second wife Anne Boleyn, whose dramatic downfall led to her execution at the Tower of London. During the upheaval of the English Civil War, Starborough Castle was demolished by order of Oliver Cromwell, but a small folly was built from the ruins and the moat survives today.

In more recent times, Winston Churchill may also have passed through the town – Chartwell, his home for 40 years, is just a couple of miles up the road. So, while Edenbridge may be small and unassuming, it is full of places and tales of great historical value, not to mention the stories of many ordinary folk who have lived here or passed through, and whose lives are no less interesting or valuable. More than that, though, it is home.

Hever Castle, which had fallen into disrepair, was beautifully restored by the Astor family after they bought it in the early 1900s. Millions of pounds were poured into the place and local craftsman were employed to ensure that everything was done to the highest standards. The marshland that surrounded the castle was landscaped and transformed into a stunning Italian garden, with walkways leading to antique statues and garden ornaments, pergolas covered with grapevines and wisteria, and nostalgic rose gardens. At the end of the gardens is a 38-acre lake, which was dug by hand and took over two years to complete, with 800 men working day and night. The river Eden, running north of the castle, was moved and diverted to fill the lake. This was a labour of love, and the castle soon became a very popular tourist attraction. It is a local treasure, with thousands visiting each year to walk in the footsteps of the former Queen of England, Anne Boleyn.

I regularly visit the castle and gardens and when I do, I try to imagine the history the stone walls bore witness to. I think about everyone who lived, worked or visited, and all the experiences they may have had. I think in particular about all the gardeners who have worked there over the years, getting to know the grounds and passing their knowledge of the landscape down through generations. And I consider, too, the wildlife they have shared it with. It's lovely to think that you can trace the history of these gardens, from over a hundred years ago right up until today, when there is still a dedicated team working to keep the grounds thriving.

I can't help but smile when I notice the resident robins in the castle grounds singing on the wall leading out of the blue garden, going about their business and ignoring the crowds of people. Perhaps the ancestors of these very robins befriended Anne Boleyn or someone in her family. No doubt the birds of the time became familiar with the Astor family's workers as they dug the lake, and as the landscapers transformed the marshlands into the stunning Italian gardens. I like to try to imagine what used to be. I used to work at Starborough Castle, and I often tried to visualize the hive of activity there must have been when they built it, and the people who lived there down the centuries. Today, a small folly sits quietly on an island. I have spent many an hour there, learning photography, and rubbing shoulders with the ghosts of the past. I wonder if any of the robins and gardeners forged relationships as close as mine and Bob's. So many stories of 'unremarkable lives' from the past go untold, and I always ponder what we've missed by not hearing them. It's easy to forget that history isn't just about humans – it's about the natural world too, and our relationship to it.

The grounds of Hever Castle are not far from the garden where I work, so I often question if any of its more 'regal' robins could be related to the robins I have known over the years. After all, they are not far away from where my story, and Bob's, begins.

* * *

My own relationship with robins started back in 2014 when I was tending one of my regular jobs in Edenbridge. As a gardener by trade, I would naturally get to know the feathered friends in the garden. They would boldly investigate what I was doing, especially when I turned the soil in the veg garden or was digging up weeds in the flowerbeds.

I worked two days a week in Bob's garden, and elsewhere for the other three days. I had befriended robins over that time, or rather they had befriended me – it was difficult to tell which! All of them lived in the same garden apart from one, 'Star', who lived at Starborough Castle. The first robin I met I named 'Robin', in 2014, and it was my close encounters with Robin that encouraged me to learn photography. I often liken photography to fishing: there's the same buzz of anticipation, the not knowing what you might catch – even though you know what you're aiming for! I was instantly hooked by the thrill of it, and the satisfying feeling when you finally get the shot you're after.

I started sharing my photos and later videos on social media, and in 2015 I created my 'Putman and Robin' Facebook and Instagram accounts (from my surname and the name of my first robin friend). I never expected it to become a significant part of my life or my work – I simply enjoyed learning photography and learning all about the robins, and wanted to share it all with like-minded people who loved robins too.

It wasn't until 5 November 2019 that I first met Bob in the garden. He was perched on the branch of a plum tree, and as I approached him, camera in hand, I took his photo.

I'd known seven robins before Bob came along, and they all disappeared within a year of our meeting. I never knew what happened to them, and I'm not ashamed to say that I found it emotionally taxing getting to know them but then losing them. Robins are wild and free, and so you don't always get closure when they suddenly vanish. So when Bob came along, I made the conscious decision that I would not try to befriend him. I'd simply photograph him and keep my distance. Well, it didn't quite work out that way as Bob had other ideas! He followed me everywhere and I couldn't help but get to know him. Before I knew it, we were best friends.

He loved the camera, was very photogenic, and I took thousands of photos of him, many of which I have shared with our followers on social media. Bob arrived a few months before the start of the Covid-19 pandemic. I was able to continue working at the job in Edenbridge during this time, and Bob became a lifeline for many who followed us. I shared photos, videos and live footage of Bob during Covid, and both my Facebook and Instagram pages grew rapidly, with followers from all over the world enjoying his antics. Bob helped me through some difficult times in my personal life, and I helped him too – we helped each other in different ways. Sharing Bob with the world also gave me a sense of purpose. He provided a feel-good factor during uncertain times, showing us how the natural world carries on, and offering hope that the human world would do so again too. I love working outdoors and getting to spend every day in nature, especially as I know that many people have to spend their working lives indoors under artificial lights. When you don't have the chance to get out into nature regularly it can be easy to forget how beautiful it is and the benefits it can bring you. I hoped that by sharing my encounters with Bob I was letting others see the possibilities of the outdoors and of gardening, and might even encourage them to seek out more time in nature.

Bob remained a wild bird, but he trusted me completely. We had a mutual respect, and, unlike the other robins before him, Bob stayed for over three years! I feel confident in saying that he must be the most famous robin in the world. With hundreds of thousands of followers worldwide, he even has his own collection of signed photos from celebrities who follow my 'Putman and Robin' account. One little bird did all that.

* * *

But things soon began to change. It started as a normal day at work. It was mid-April, the sun was shining, the birds were singing, and spring was well underway. The only difference from previous years was that Bob no longer occupied his territory, the plum tree, which he had surrendered to Bobbin and Bobette – two younger robins, male and female, the female of which I believed to be Bob's daughter – after losing his partner, Betty, in February.

Bob stayed close to the house, foraging in the flowerbeds for food and using the ornamental yew trees and larger shrubs as shelter. That day, I spent a lot of my time working on the flowerbeds near the house, digging them over and clearing the weeds. Bob stayed close and spent most of his time with me. I even took a selfie with him as he perched on a large ornamental urn in the flowerbed. He was comfortable with me being in his space, so I leaned nearer to him and took our photo using my phone. At that point, I had no reason to think that I wouldn't see him the next time I came to work.

When it was time for me to go home, though, I remember thinking how small Bob looked as he stood in the middle of the lawn. For some reason, his diminutive frame really stood out to me that day – robins are only around 4 inches in height. I watched him as he saw me pull away in my van and drive out through the gate. I had an uneasy feeling that this could be the last time I saw him.

Days passed with no sign of Bob. I looked for him everywhere; any slight movement in the hedge would grab my attention. When passing through his territory, I'd look eagerly at his favourite perches – the branch on the plum tree, the picket fence, the top of the yew tree, and in the mixed hedge where he'd so often greet me or wait for me – only to be met with emptiness, and my memories of our time together.

Where Bob had always made it a place full of surprises and companionship, work became for me a place of sadness, and the feeling of loss was intense. It felt like a numbness had engulfed me, an overwhelming feeling of knowing there was nothing I could do, along with the hope that the next time I looked he'd be there, looking back at me. But he was nowhere to be seen.

It was the same feeling I'd had when I'd lost a good friend, Steve, with whom I'd workcd in a games factory many years before. I was at work when another friend called me to tell me he had passed away, and although he didn't work with me anymore, as he'd left for a new job months before, I still struggled to continue to work that day. It was a big shock. All I could think about were the happy times we'd shared when we'd worked together, standing alongside one another and working on benches under the skylights, right by the shutter door of the woodwork department. We'd do the PopMaster radio quiz together in the morning, then have our deep and meaningful conversations in the afternoon. Or we'd simply spend time together, having a laugh as we did our work. All those happy memories turned to sadness for me as soon as I learned of his passing.

On one occasion, Steve and I had an unexpected visitor in the factory. It was a hot summer's day, and the doors in the woodwork department were wide open. Steve was working on the bench next to me, directly in front of the shutter door, when a huge dragonfly came flying in. It was bright blue, with transparent wings, and it flew straight up to the skylights. We could hear it repeatedly crashing into the glass of the closed window as it tried to get out, but the only way out was back through the open door! This went on until it became apparent that the dragonfly wasn't going to make its escape, so we decided to rescue it. There were tall shelves full of stock from floor to ceiling in the factory so we had large ladders on wheels in our workspace. Steve fetched one – it easily reached the skylight – and positioned it for me to climb up to the dragonfly. I made my way up with no idea of how, exactly, I was going to manage it. The insect was pretty much the size of my hand and I didn't want to just make a grab for it in case I hurt it.

When I got within reach, I instinctively held out my hand and rubbed my index and middle finger together, kind of mimicking the sound its wings make as it flies. I've no idea why I did that, but it worked, and the dragonfly immediately flew to my hand and landed on my index finger! I made my way back down the ladder to Steve, and we walked outside with the dragonfly still perched on my finger. It was a magnificent-looking creature, with its wings shimmering multiple colours in the sunlight and its metallic blue body. As if it knew it was being rescued, it sat calmly on my finger until I raised my hand, and it flew away.

At the time, we both felt a great sense of satisfaction, and astonishment, that the dragonfly had so willingly trusted us and allowed us to rescue it. Long afterwards, we would often reflect fondly on that moment, and on the safe release of the dragonfly back outside.

Just as it did with Steve's passing, it took me a long time to process Bob's disappearance. Deep down, I knew that Bob was gone and that looking for him in the usual places was in vain. I also knew that Bobbin and Bobette now occupied his territory as a pair; they had done so even before he'd disappeared. I'd already built up some sort of relationship with Bobbin and Bobette. I never considered them to be a replacement for Bob, but they certainly helped me deal with his disappearance, and I never held any resentment towards them for taking Bob's territory. Indeed, it was the fact that Bob was so tolerant of them when they were living in the hedge next to him and his partner Betty that made me think one of them was his offspring from the previous year.

Betty's disappearance was, in my opinion, the reason for Bob giving up his territory to Bobbin and Bobette. I don't believe they had anything to do with that, and by occupying the territory to survive they are just doing what comes naturally to them. Even if Bob hadn't disappeared, it was inevitable that I would build some sort of relationship with them. When a robin (or two or three) decides they want to know you, they become very difficult to ignore.

As much as I like my job and love the garden, if it hadn't been for Bobbin and Bobette, I think I may have considered looking for work elsewhere. Their inquisitiveness and antics made me want to keep returning to the garden to check in on them and follow their movements. But I have to admit that it was the chance, however small, that Bob could come back in the autumn after the breeding season and annual moult, that still preoccupied me, and is definitely part of what convinced me to stay.

# Chapter Two

# Bobbin and Bobette

Spring 2023. Bobbin is very talkative; he follows me to the edges of his territory and waits for my return, just like Bob used to do. Bob would chatter to me too, but he would more often than not use clicking noises to get my attention, whereas Bobbin uses more of a gentle twitter, a continuous, soft melody. I love how the robins are so different in their ways. I knew they were here to stay, so I had to give them names to make it easy for our followers on social media to identify them. I honestly don't think I would have named any of the robins I've known over the years if I wasn't sharing their journey like this. I would have simply enjoyed knowing them.

I can't remember why I settled for the names Bobbin and Bobette. I normally ask our followers to help name the robins, but not this time. I just wanted to give them names with 'Bob' in them. For a time, before Bob disappeared, we had Bob,

Bobbin and Bobette all together at once. As much as I missed Bob, I couldn't help smiling when I saw Bobbin – he always had a cheerful manner. I'd known him for no more than four months, and I could photograph and film him easily: just like Bob, he showed little or no fear of me. I always filmed him using my phone. Mobile cameras are so good, and so convenient for filming spontaneously when the robins do something funny or fascinating. It just goes to show that anyone can try their hand at wildlife photography, even if they only have a smartphone. It's much easier than with a big, clumsy DSLR camera (although I do still use mine for high-resolution photos).

One day in late April, Bobbin was twittering away on a branch as I approached. He continued happily, ignoring me completely, even though I was standing right in front of him. This was very familiar to me, as Bob would do exactly the same: continuing to do whatever he was doing regardless of whether I was there or not. For years, I was able to film and document him, knowing that my presence didn't alter his behaviour. It is one of the things I most cherish about the unique relationship between gardener and robin: that they become so used to you that they act as if you aren't there, allowing you an insight into their lives that not many other people are granted. I always saw this as a gift, and was very grateful to be able to experience it.

As Bobbin was singing, a soft continuous twitter, he started slowly, but very deliberately, swaying and moving his head from side to side in time with his melodic song. It could, I thought, be some sort of territorial dance, to show off his red breast to a potential rival and protect his and Bobette's patch of land – though I didn't actually see another robin nearby. Another, perhaps more likely, explanation could be that he was showing off to Bobette. Robins have a relatively long courtship period, which does involve singing and the male feeding the female. It certainly seemed as if Bobbin was saying, 'Look at me! Aren't I great at singing and dancing!?' His cheerful little song and dance really made me smile. I'd filmed Bob for over three years and although I had heard him singing this sort of song many times before, I'd never seen him dance like that. This was something completely new to me – yet another thing to learn about robins. So of course I shared the video with our followers on social media.

I was constantly getting messages asking, 'What happened to Bob?' 'Where's Bob?' Or comments like, 'Bobbin can never replace Bob!' But I was never sharing Bobbin or Bobette in order to replace Bob. I simply got to know them, and their story naturally continued on my social media. And, as I've mentioned, since Bobette was probably Bob's daughter, this was a way to continue his legacy too. It did get a little hard being asked the same questions all the time. Bob was already on my mind every day, and I myself didn't know what had happened or where he was. But really, it just showed how much love there was for Bob the robin. I hoped that sharing this video of Bobbin might lift the mood a bit for my followers, as seeing him showing off had brightened my own day, reminding me how much fun there was to be had in the garden with the new robins and their different personalities.

* * *

Bobbin and Bobette are a close couple; Bobette is never far from Bobbin unless she is on the nest. It is so important to leave a robin, or any bird nest, well alone. Although I might have a good idea of where a nest is, I will never look for it or go near it intentionally. Robins like to keep their nests secret. If they feel a nest has been discovered, they might abandon it or even force their fledglings to fledge before they are ready. Of course, I don't need to describe what the outcome of that could be! No matter how well I know the robins, or how much they trust me, this is a rule I stick to: I will never look for the nest.

Bobette certainly knows who I am, although she keeps her distance. It could be that female robins are naturally more cautious than the males, though this is based only on my observation of the robins in the garden. Male and female robins differ more in behaviour than in appearance, but it is still difficult to tell them apart until mating season is underway, as it is now, when the male robins become the providers – and Bobbin is proving to be a great provider for Bobette!

Male robins feed the females during breeding, which helps to strengthen their bond and provides the female with nutrients for when she is egg laying. The female will beg the male for food with a shrieking call as well as by fluttering her wings. This is sometimes followed by another shrieking sound, slightly different to the first, immediately after the male feeds her – a sort of 'thank you'. The female will incubate and hatch the eggs, and both male and female will forage for food to provide for the hatchlings. When the young fledge the nest, the male will continue to feed them for a couple of weeks or so, and the female will often start on the next clutch, with new eggs being laid shortly after the fledglings depart. This will go on throughout the breeding season, as both male and female work tirelessly to provide for and raise their young, sometimes having up to three broods a year! This teamwork helps maximize the survival rate of their young. The more they have the better, as mortality rate is high in young robins. My thoughts often turn to Bob, hoping he's just over the hedge somewhere providing for his new family too.

* * *

As May arrives, the apple trees and pear trees are coming into bloom, the hawthorn hedges are white with blossom, and butterflies and bees flock to the garden. They love the blooms as they provide the nectar they need for energy. Everything feels alive. The garden is at its most beautiful, and it is my favourite time of year! With the anticipation of new life and warmer weather, the buzzing of bees and insects, what's not to love?

Food is plentiful for the robins now and they need me less and less: a fresh bug of some sort is far more nutritious and satisfying than anything I could provide for them. They're wild animals, after all, and it is important that I'm just a supplementer not a provider. I don't want them to rely on me, as they're more than capable of fending for themselves. I just like to give them a little help from time to time. I do leave small piles of mealworms, suet pellets and birdseeds on posts in the hawthorn hedge, and it doesn't go unnoticed by other birds and animals. I don't leave silly amounts – just enough to help them through the day if they want it.

I notice other garden birds queuing up in the hedge, waiting for me to back up to a safe distance so that they can help themselves.

A female blackbird is never far away, her nervous alarm call, which seemingly goes off at random, often causing the other birds to scatter. She certainly knows who I am and will sometimes come close knowing I will drop a mealworm or two in her direction. She will even compete with the robins to see who can get the mealworm first, but of course there is enough for them all. I can also see the blue tits, great tits, sparrows and nuthatches following as I make my way down the garden, flitting from hedge to shrub or shrub to hedge as they all enjoy an easy meal too. The great tits and blue tits are rarely far away, cautiously watching from a branch or two above me when I am interacting with the robins. These birds are more wary of me because they see large mammals and humans as a threat, whereas robins are more naturally predisposed to follow and get close to people. Out in wild areas, robins are known to follow larger mammals such as deer, as the movement of these creatures leads to disturbed ground, which makes it easier for the robins to access worms and insects. They are opportunistic eaters, wherever they are! The robins in the garden, of course, also know and trust me and are therefore much bolder – they don't hesitate to get stuck in to the food I leave them while I'm still present.

This garden is a perfect home for garden birds. Looking up at the house, on your right you'll see a hawthorn hedge over 10 feet tall and over 80 feet long running down the side of the garden. Perpendicular to the hawthorn is a yew hedge which leads up to the house, creating a squared horseshoe shape that provides great protection and shelter for animals. The yew hedge is only around 4 feet high, but very compact and dense, and it provided great shelter for Bob, especially during extreme conditions. I would sometimes find him having a snooze in there during the day.

In front of the hedge is the plum tree, where I first met Bob back in 2019 and where I so often filmed him.

The hedge then snakes round in a square horseshoe shape, and surrounds a brick paved seating area with an outbuilding running parallel to it. The building offers shelter for the birds as they can easily get inside through the corrugated roof, and it is here where Bobette has her nest. One day, I heard rustling in the undergrowth and little squeaking noises coming from the floor of the hedge so I decided to investigate. That's when I discovered that the hawthorn was also home to a family of shrews! Shrews are tiny mammals with very small eyes and long snouts that give them an excellent sense of smell. They resemble mice in appearance but they are not rodents, and are in fact more closely related to moles and hedgehogs.

They are rarely seen because they usually live – just like this family – in undergrowth, leaf litter and long vegetation, but they are one of the UK's most abundant mammals. They are also difficult to see because they are absolutely tiny, with their bodies usually measuring between 2.5 and 3 inches, so spotting this group was a real treat.

Keeping very still and quiet, I crouched down to observe them scurrying back and forth along the layered parts of the hedge, which they used as a shrew highway. Happily, any fallen bird food was theirs to collect – they'd pick it up and scuttle back to the safety of their nest. The shrews were so small and moved so fast that it was difficult to keep a visual on them as they moved among fallen leaves on the floor of the hedge. But I was happy to see they'd found a home in the garden.

With the warmer weather ushering in a feeling of expectation and new hope, I decided to start sharing a photo of Bob every day on Facebook and Instagram. Since Bob's disappearance, I'd mainly been posting video footage of Bobbin and Bobette, but I wanted to hold onto the hope of Bob returning, so doing this would be my way of keeping his memory alive. I'd taken many photos of Bob over the three years I'd known him, but my photography had declined significantly since he'd gone. I just wasn't doing it anywhere near as much as I once had. The hobby, along with Bob himself, had helped me so much during difficult times, but it had faded along with Bob's leaving. I honestly don't know if Bob was the reason for that, or if it was something that was gradually happening anyway. I would still film Bobbin and Bobette with my phone camera, and continued to share the results with our followers, but my days of carrying my DSLR camera around with me everywhere was over for now.

I knew how much our followers on social media missed Bob, so I thought sharing a photo of him every day until Christmas would be a nice tribute to him. It did me good, too, as it kept me in touch with using Photoshop, and working on photos of my dear friend brought back lovely memories of him. I still held a little glimmer of hope that maybe, just maybe, Bob would come home after the breeding season was over.

* * *

Bobbin and Bobette now controlled a large territory in the garden: all the way from the house to the compost bins, which was roughly the length of a football pitch! The whole of the main garden was theirs to move freely around, and they would keep me company as I worked. At this time of year, my jobs involved neatening the edges of the flowerbeds and keeping them weed-free, and also mowing the large lawn. I used a large ride-on cylinder mower to cut the main body of the lawn, and then a small rotary mower to cut around the edges, leaving a neat finish of straight lines, which is always pleasing on the eye.

Bobbin was my main companion during this time, as Bobette spent a lot of her time on the nest. Even when she was around she was a little more reserved. Bobbin, however, would appear to me proudly – either landing on the steering wheel of the tractor mower, wheelbarrow handle or my garden fork. He'd show off his beak full of critters, spiders, flies and green caterpillars, often with them still wriggling as he held them clamped in his beak, sometimes three or four at a time! This always fascinated me: how birds can catch multiple prey, opening their beaks to catch a new victim without dropping the others! After displaying his catch, he'd go off to the nest to feed Bobette and the fledglings. Bobbin was proving to be a great dad and provider for his family.

As June began, the garden was full of colour, with the roses, echinacea, peonies, nepeta and poppies all bursting into flower. On the edge of one of the flowerbeds was a sea of poppies that had self-sown. This happens after the poppy has flowered: the head forms into a pod with many seeds, and when the head dries out the seeds rattle inside and are dispersed through the top of the pod by the wind or by animals brushing past them. The poppies create a beautiful wave of red as they blow in the wind. Seeing a photo opportunity, I placed a wooden-handled half moon – the edger I use for creating the clean edges of the flowerbed – in the ground in front of the poppies, knowing that Bobbin would likely land on the handle if I was nearby. The poppies would make a beautiful backdrop for a photo of Bobbin on the handle. This set-up and anticipation rekindled that intense, overwhelming feeling of excitement that photography had so often brought me in the past. With my camera at the ready, it didn't take long for Bobbin's curiosity to get the better of him, and he was soon perched on the handle. The resulting photographs didn't disappoint. This moment very much reignited my interest and love for photography.

* * *

The breeding season was coming to an end, and Bobbin and Bobette proved to be great parents in what I believe to have been their first breeding year. I did see their young, with their light-brown speckled breasts, keeping a safe distance in the thick of the hedges, but I did not interact with any of them as they were very shy. It's a good thing for them to be naturally cautious: who knows where their lives will take them?

For reasons unknown to me, Bobbin and Bobette moved away from the main garden and spent most of their time at the compost bins halfway down the other end of the garden. These 'bins' are actually three bays built from wooden planks. They're a good size for the large lawn and are crucial for good compost. The first bay is often filled to the brim with grass cuttings by the end of the year, and the other two with the previous two years' cuttings: I like to have a rotation system to get good compost. In the spring I will use the third bay's compost – containing the oldest cuttings – and put it on the flowerbeds and veg garden. I'll then empty the other two bays' content into the next bay along. This helps the material to compost better, also freeing up the first bay ready for the cuttings when mowing starts in spring. It's a simple system – one that anyone with the space can easily adopt – but it works wonders for the growth and health of the garden.

Near the bins, halfway down the garden, is a stock fence with a gate in the middle that separates the main garden from an orchard on the other side. The orchard is roughly the size of a football pitch, with apple, pear and plum trees, and there is a lake at the bottom with fields beyond that. The bins sit in front of a dense undergrowth that hosts a mixture of wild roses, brambles, blackthorns and pretty much everything with thorns. Next to the bins sit two large trees as well as a small hawthorn tree and a large hedge running to the left, heading towards a small willow woodland before the lake.

I can see why the robins favoured this spot as they were very well protected from predators, such as sparrowhawks or anything else that might fancy taking on a robin. They had access to easy meals, too, the compost bins being full of worms just under the surface, and the decomposition attracting flies and other bugs. I guess the compost area proved an ideal place for going through their annual moult, a process that makes them vulnerable as they are less able to fly and less able to insulate themselves from the cold.

It wasn't long before they started to look a little worse for wear as patches of feathers started to fall out, slowly being replaced by new ones. The robins still interacted with me, and I was able to film them and share what was happening to them on my socials – they seemed to still trust me despite their increased vulnerability. But their new feathers eventually pushed their way through to replace the old ones, and they were ready to take on the winter to come.

As winter loomed, after moulting by the compost bins, Bobbin and Bobette parted company; Bobette went back into Bob's territory and occupied the plum tree area, though not all the way up to the house as Bob had done. Bobbin remained by the bins and the bottom half of the mixed hedge. Though they stayed separate from this point on, I kept in touch with them both, ensuring they had plenty of food, especially during the cold days running up to Christmas. Bob never moved territory to moult – he always stayed in the mixed hedge and in his plum tree – so this was all new to me. It also gave me renewed hope when Bobbin and Bobette vacated Bob's territory to moult that maybe, just maybe, Bob might return. With the territory he had occupied just before he vanished now vacant there was nothing to stop him coming back. So if he is just over the hedge somewhere, maybe he'll be coming home soon.

# Chapter Three

# The Winter Spell

On the last day of 2023, 31 December, my wife and I took a final walk of the year with our dogs. Our New Year's Eve was also spent with Dave the crow, a familiar friend. I'd known Dave since 2020, and he'd often join us for a walk when we took the dogs for a run to their favourite spot near where we live. Dave and Mrs Dave, as I call her, occupy the territory we pass on our walk. Dave is able to recognize both my car and my van, so he quickly made himself known by landing at my feet as soon as we turned up! My dogs Pup and Saa are not bothered by the presence of Dave at all, and they'll all happily run along together, often with Dave hopping along next to me.

Although in folklore crows have long been an omen of dark magic, bad luck or even death, they are very friendly, and are among the happiest of all the birds in the UK to share spaces with humans. They are notably curious, intelligent and observant of human behaviour. One scientific study has even suggested that crows have reasoning skills equivalent to those of a seven-year-old human! It has been proven that crows are able to recognize individual human faces, and if you search 'CrowTok', you'll find thousands of videos of people who've befriended them. Just as I have built a relationship of trust and curiosity with Bob and the other robins, people all over the world have done the same with crows. Dave, for his part, has always shown an interest in me and the dogs, and I have always been happy to see him.

That New Year's Eve was a quintessential British winter's day: very wet with puddles and mud everywhere – not that it bothered the dogs, as they love to run whatever the weather. I called the boys over for a treat, and Pup, Saa and Dave lined up patiently, waiting for me to give them each a dog bone biscuit. My dogs can't eat theirs quick enough – they want to get on with their walk, with plenty of running and smells that need investigating – but Dave will take his treat and fly away with it, probably burying it somewhere to be eaten later. And although Mrs Dave always hangs back and keeps her distance, I don't forget about her either. I gently threw a treat in her direction and she eagerly picked it up and took it away.

The year started the same way as it ended, with a nice long, albeit wet, walk with the dogs, and of course with Dave the crow joining us. The next day I visited the robins. I found Bobbin in the orchard perched on the branch of a small crab-apple tree. The tree was still holding onto its fruit from the summer so it was the perfect spot for Bobbin to get food in the cold. With the rain falling, I gave Bobbin some mealworms to help him through the day, and filmed him on my phone to share with our followers on social media.

The rain quickly yielded to colder weather and by the middle of January we had snow – it was bitterly cold! Just as Bob did four years prior, Bobbin left the safety of his territory on the other side of the plum tree to join me on the pergola. Bobette occupied this part of the garden, and although they'd been a breeding pair the previous spring, she would still defend her territory and possibly fight him off if she saw him, so Bobbin was taking a risk. Robins are regarded as fiercely territorial, as they will defend their territory all year round. However, it's something of a misconception that they are more aggressive than other garden birds, who behave in similar ways. The idea of robins being particularly vicious is perhaps an overcorrection of their cute, fluffy reputation from Christmas cards and story books – something that most other garden birds don't have to contend with to quite the same degree! Some people say that robins will fight to the death in order to protect their patches, and I am sure that this has probably happened, but I have never seen any serious physical confrontations among them, just short skirmishes resulting in one quickly backing down. In fact, to me they seem very good at resolving conflicts with nonviolent territorial behaviour, such as singing. I've often witnessed sparrows squabbling as they battle their way through the hedges, and blue tits seeing off other blue tits as they defend their territories, especially during spring. Such aggression is all about survival and you'll find that many bird species are highly territorial, not just the robin.

Even so, getting an injury from fighting was very possible if Bobbin was seen to be invading Bobette's territory, and this was the last thing he'd want in these freezing conditions. Life for the robins was all about surviving the winter now.

I had an odd feeling of déjà vu as I worked in the snow. I was 8 feet up a ladder on top of the pergola, pruning the wisteria and roses. The snow was over an inch deep on the wooden structure, and it soaked my gloves and went up my sleeves as I stretched to reach branches to prune. Bob and I had supported each other through many winter seasons, and as the cold bit into my toes and hands, I recalled those past years and that feeling of togetherness as we fought the same elements.

Bobbin sat there, his feet resting on top of the snow as he wasn't heavy enough to sink into it. And yet the cold was a far more intense battle for him than it was for me. He didn't get to go home to a nice warm house at the end of the day but would have to stay out and endure the freezing night to come. There are places of shelter here for him and the other birds, like the large outbuilding with the corrugated roof. There is also dense vegetation, such as yew hedges and trees as well as mixed hedges and large shrubs, so I knew he could get out of the extreme weather if he needed to. I offered him mealworms, which he gladly gobbled up, since food is so much harder to find at this time of the year. The ground is frozen solid, and the bugs are safely tucked away, waiting for warmer days and out of the reach of a hungry robin. With all the fallen fruit now gone, it is a battle of opportunity and endurance.

Robins are members of the Old World

flycatcher family, Muscicapidae, and will eat a variety of different foods, though this name gives a strong hint as to what their favourite is! I've watched the robins I've known hunt and catch a variety of different bugs on the wing, from bees to flies, and I even saw Bobette catch and eat a small dragonfly, which was quite a mouthful for her! They will often join me as I dig over the ground, either weeding the flowerbeds or the veg garden, and they'll help themselves to any critters I uncover: worms, centipedes and, especially, spiders, which they love! But the robins will adjust to the seasons, and they will quite happily eat fruit, too, if it's available. I've seen them eat yew berries, holly berries, hawthorn berries and crab apples: they are very adaptable and the ultimate survivor. During a single cold night, a robin can lose up to 10 per cent of its body weight just trying to keep warm, so a prolonged cold spell can prove deadly. It's easy to see why Bobbin, probably trying to replenish fat reserves during the daytime, would risk a telling-off from Bobette to come and spend time with me. Of course, I do leave food for the birds at different feeding stations in the garden – on spent fence posts in the mixed hedge, under the yew hedge and certain shrubs, sheltered in areas of safety – so the birds can eat without the worry of being attacked by a sparrowhawk or other birds of prey. I couldn't help but smile as Bobbin kept me company, noticing how his behaviour echoed that of Bob's. I sure missed my dear friend, but Bobbin's antics kept me going, even through the biting cold days.

The snow didn't last long and was all gone within a few days, although it remained very cold. It was the time of year for me to prune the apple trees in the orchard, thinning back last year's growth and any dead branches to improve light and air circulation to the canopy. The compost bins back onto the orchard, so I was often joined by Bobbin as he'd seemingly supervise every cut as I made my way from tree to tree.

I'd noticed a change with the robins. Even though it was still January, it was the time of the year when they'd start pairing up, ready for spring. For whatever reason, Bobbin and Bobette did not pair up this time, and I noticed Bobbin with a new partner. The plum tree marked the territorial divide: Bobette and her new partner occupied the top half of the garden, from the house to the plum tree; and Bobbin and his partner had the bottom half, from the other side of the plum tree, and the other half of the mixed hedge, down to the compost bins.

Usually, male robins attract mates in late winter or early spring by loudly singing. But it's not always the female who moves territory, sometimes the male robin will join the female in her territory, and they will occupy and defend it together. Once a partner has been found, they establish and strengthen their bond by feeding the female. This is often the easiest way to tell males and females apart: if you see one robin feeding another, the bird being fed will be female, and the one doing the feeding will be male.

Generally, though, it is difficult to identify the sex of the robins. Male and female robins, to my eye, look identical. Though I'd seen Bob with Betty on many occasions, it was always from a distance as Betty would rarely come close to me. Bobbin and his new partner, Ruby, now offered a very good opportunity to study them at close quarters for visible differences, as they were happy to be right in front of me. I have seen comments from people on my posts saying that only male robins have the red breast. Of course, this is not true at all. I do wonder where this incorrect information comes from as so many people seem to believe it!

From what I can gather, if you go back a generation or two, this seems to be what people were taught at school. A possible explanation is that people confused dunnocks with female robins. Dunnocks can be found in very similar environments to robins, and do have a tendency to follow robins around. They are of a similar size, and all brown, so I can see how the confusion could have arisen. Robin fledglings are all brown too, but with speckled chests, so perhaps they have also have been mistaken for adult females? But from all my time spent with the robins, I can say with certainty that both the males and the females have distinctive red breasts.

Another method of telling robins apart that is often cited in social media comments, but one that is, in my opinion, unreliable, is a difference in the head cap, above the beak and eyes where the orange changes to brown. I have seen comments saying that the female has a V-shaped cap, while the male's is more of a U shape. There is some weight to this, and I have observed a V shape on Bobette's head, but it is very difficult to see and could be easily misidentified. Other comments I've seen include: 'the orange of the breast of the female doesn't go down as far as the male's'; 'the male robin is bigger than the female'; 'the female has a white tip on the end of her wings whereas the male doesn't'; 'the orange of the male breast is brighter and more vibrant than that of a female robin'; and 'only the male robin sings'. But I could point out exceptions to almost all of these statements in what I have observed in the robins in the garden.

I am very confident that the two birds standing right in front of me are indeed male and female, as two males certainly would not tolerate each other, and I know for sure that Bobbin is male! I have looked at the pair of them in great detail, have photographed and filmed them, but I have seen no obvious differences at all: the orange breast is the same, it is extremely hard to see any real difference in the head shape, and there are no white tips on her wings. They look identical. I know who is who simply because I know their characteristics and know them as individuals. The only reliable way of telling a male robin from a female is that in the spring, the female robin will call the male robin, asking him to feed her.

Once this period of courtship is over, the female then gets to work building the nest out of leaves and grass, usually in a bush or tree, sometimes in an outbuilding, where she will lay and hatch the eggs after mating.

Bobbin's new partner was never far away from him, just like Bobette the previous year. She quickly learned that I was no threat to her as she watched Bobbin interacting with me from a safe distance. Halfway down the garden in their territory I placed a wooden-handled fork and a half moon side by side and I left them there. This would now become where I would meet and interact with Bobbin and his partner. I thought it likely that this new female would be making frequent appearances on my social media, now that she had paired up with Bobbin, so decided to ask my followers to help name her. 'Ruby' was the winner, and so Ruby she became! The area is well sheltered and protected from the wind, with the hedges offering safety from predators. It didn't take long before Bobbin was perched on one handle and Ruby on the other – they never perched on the same handle at the same time as they liked, in these early days of their relationship, to keep some distance between them. I filmed them using my phone, as usual, sharing daily updates to my 'Putman and Robin' followers on social media. But I also photographed them using my DSLR camera, after Bobbin had reignited my passion for photography last summer.

Bobbin, being so bold and confident, would often make photographing him tricky as he liked to get involved by perching on the lens of my camera, even when I was holding it trying to take a photo! One time I set my camera up on the tripod in front of the wooden-handled tools, which were still placed in the ground as perches. I had the camera focused on Ruby as she was on one of the perches, and I used the camera's back screen to focus on her. I was then able to film the back screen using my phone, showing Ruby on the screen with Bobbin perched on top of the camera seemingly acting as a director! It was an amusing moment and a very cherished memory. I shared the video with my followers on social media, and the clip reached over 1.2 million views on Instagram! While I'm confident that Bob trusted me completely, he still kept a respectful distance most of the time. Bobbin, however, didn't trust me as Bob had done, but he really didn't mind where he put himself, and he was always happily in the thick of it with me, with no worries about boundaries. Bob and Bobbin were very different characters. It's lovely to see how individual robins are.

* * *

Digging over the vegetable garden is one of those jobs that will make you sweat even on the coldest winter day. The veg garden is situated behind the first section of mixed hedge, so I go through the archway dividing the hedges to access it. It is a large area, built using sleepers, two high all the way round, filled with good, easy-to-dig soil. At one end, to the left as I look at the veg plot, there are raspberry canes, two or three deep, running the width of the plot. In front of them to the right is a sizeable rhubarb plant; both the raspberries and rhubarb come back each year, so they stay where they are. The next row features large redcurrant and blackcurrant bushes, standing around 4 feet tall, with a gooseberry bush at the end. All these plants stay all year round. The rest of the plot is used to grow runner beans, potatoes, French beans, spinach and other veg, all planted seasonally. During the winter this section of the plot is empty, and it needs nutrients added to help it replenish from the previous growing season and make ready for the next.

Using a garden fork, I dug the soil a spit deep (a spade depth) and as I turned it, I broke it up to make it loose and airy. My efforts didn't go unnoticed, and Bobbin soon joined me, hopping around by my feet as I worked, gobbling up any worms or bugs I uncovered. Repetitively turning the soil does make my back ache nowadays, so I like to have a little break every now and then for a rest or a coffee.

I sat down on one of the sleepers with my legs stretched out in front of me to help ease my back. When Bobbin perched himself on the toe of my boot, I took my phone from my pocket and started filming him. Saa, my dog, was lying roughly 10 feet away in front of me, too, so the video had Bobbin on my boot, with Saa in the background, happily minding his own business. I offered Bobbin a mealworm, which he took from me contentedly and ate where he sat, still on my boot. I posted the video on my Instagram account, and the clip gained over 6.1 million views! I'm not sure if it was Bobbin on my boot or Saa in the background that made it so successful – probably a combination of both.

I'm a lover of all animals but my dogs are something special. As I mentioned earlier, I have two dogs, Pup and Saa. Pup is the oldest. I've had him since he was a pup and he is now 13 years old. Saa is a rescue dog, from Many Tears Animal Rescue in Wales, and he's roughly eight or nine years old – I don't know his exact age. They are both Border collies of sorts. Saa is the more traditional-looking, with long black and white hair, and Pup has short black and white hair. Both are large for their breed, and they enjoy coming to work with me. As an energetic breed, they need to be out and about, so it's great that I can offer them that with the work I do. Pup got his name simply because I am not very original with names: he was a puppy when I got him, so I called him Pup from the off and the name just stuck! His favourite pastime is waiting by the back door for my customer to come out of the house, hoping he'll get a biscuit – which he often does! Saa got his name from the rescue centre he came from, and, as he started working with me the day he moved in, being able to call him effectively was a priority, while renaming him wasn't. In any case, Pup's name shows how good I am with names, so Saa kept his! Saa will stay close to me all day as he likes to know where I am at all times, but if he hears that back door open, then he's also gone like a shot. There is no way he's missing out on a treat!

Saa loves where I work. And his favourite spot is at the bottom of the garden where there's a lake that has a jetty, a decked platform leading into the water. I feed the fish from the jetty, and Saa loves nothing more than to watch them. He watches with great enthusiasm when I throw food in, and some of the fish are of a good size, maybe nearing 20 pounds or more: there are common carp, mirror carp and a couple of koi carp. I've known the fish for over 15 years, and it's been a pleasure to watch them grow. There's one I can even identify because it always blows bubbles when it feeds, sucking the food from below the surface. It must have a slightly deformed mouth, as the number of bubbles is far more than from any other fish, making it easily identifiable when it is feeding!

Saa has been known to sometimes disappear while I'm working, without me noticing. But when I do, I know where I'll find him. One hot summer's day Saa went missing, so I made my way to the lake and there he was, swimming about with the fish! He likes to follow them and try to get a good look at them. Saa didn't know I was there, and I thought him swimming about would make a good film, so I used the camera on my phone. Not long into filming, Saa got right up to a fish, and as he put his nose closer he startled it. As it thrashed to get away the fish slapped Saa around the face with its tail! I couldn't help but laugh as Saa paused there with a shocked look on his face, wondering what had just happened. But he quickly shook it off and got back to business, looking for more fish. The best thing is that I managed to capture it all on film! Saa is living his best life, and I am so pleased we adopted him from the rescue centre. There are so many animals in desperate need of a good home.

Bobbin and Saa were obviously a photogenic pair for my social media following, and that moment of joy when our post went viral took me back in my mind to the days of Bob and how he was such a loved bird. His whereabouts, however, remained a mystery. Pup and Saa are always with me at my place of work, and the robins accept them into their territories just as they have accepted me. They rarely take any notice of each other, though. Maybe one of my dogs will turn his head as a bold robin hops by within feet of him, but there is no real interest from either party.

## Chapter Four

# The Disappearance of Bobbin

While preparing to publish my first book about Bob, I received a large cardboard cut-out of the book cover from my publisher, as a prop for announcing the publication date. I was quite confident that if I placed the prop in the right place, next to the hedge where Bobbin and Ruby lived, that Bobbin wouldn't be able to resist coming to see what I was up to and that he'd land on it – perfect for a photo to share with our followers on social media to announce the release of Bob's book. On Friday 8 March 2024, I drove to the garden and got there just after sunrise. I made my way eagerly to the hedge where I'd so often meet Bobbin and Ruby, with camera bag on my back, prop in one hand and camera tripod in the other. I was full of confidence that we'd have a successful photoshoot – I just couldn't wait to get started! But, when I got to the hedge, I was greeted with nothing but silence. No sign of Bobbin or

Ruby. This wasn't completely unusual. They have a habit of seeming to have disappeared, or of staying out of sight when they don't want to be seen, and then suddenly reappearing. So I wasn't too worried at first.

I stood the prop in front of the hedge, thinking that at any second Bobbin would appear. But there was nothing. I placed my camera onto the tripod and set it at the right distance to photograph the prop, ready for Bobbin to land on it. I waited and waited, but still there was nothing. This was unusual, so I decided to go and look for both Bobbin and Ruby. After a while, an hour or so of searching in all the places they could be – the compost bins, the vegetable garden, the orchard, the willow trees and all the hedges – I eventually found Ruby. She was always a little warier of me than Bobbin was, just like Bobette, and less likely to come flying out to greet me. Ruby was keeping a low profile, tucked away deep in the hawthorn hedge, right next to where I'd set up my camera. She was so difficult to spot it's possible that she'd been there the whole time. This was a little unnerving because Bobbin was usually near her, but there was no sign of him. I carried on searching but I never found him.

The following week my search for Bobbin continued, but it was in vain. Bobbin had always been full of life and very interactive, so I didn't hold out any real hope of finding him. Sadly, I strongly suspected that he'd been predated. The greatest likelihood is that a sparrowhawk had got him, as I had seen one in the area on many occasions. The Eurasian sparrowhawk is a small bird of prey, a specialized ambush predator that predominantly hunts garden birds such as sparrows, tits, starlings and thrushes, or birds of a similar size, using stealth and speed to hunt and kill its prey. It is one of the most common birds of prey in Europe and not to be messed with.

However, I had other theories in mind too. Robins are small birds, roughly the size of a sparrow, and they are primarily ground feeders, foraging among the undergrowth for insects and worms. This leaves them vulnerable to attack from ground animals, including, sadly, animals introduced by humans, especially the domestic cat. Cats are responsible for killing millions of birds in the UK each year, but it's a huge problem all over the world.

We all love to see birds, and many people buy bird food to attract their feathered friends to the feeders in their gardens. They set out with the best of intentions, trying to do their bit to help bird populations, but if they have a cat, they are unwittingly attracting birds to a garden where an apex predator is waiting. I've seen comments on my social media posts along the lines of 'my cat brought a robin in yesterday, sad, but I guess it's just nature'. I am never sure if comments like these are genuine, or are simply looking for a reaction, but I can assure you that this predation is not 'just nature'. The threat to garden birds from domestic cats is a man-made problem. It's our choice whether we have a cat or not, so it's our responsibility to do whatever we can to stop them from hunting our wildlife.

To be clear, I am not against people owning cats. I love cats: they have been here for centuries, and have been keeping rodent populations under control for just as long. I also know that they come with all sorts of different personalities. In fact, I grew up in a house full of them as my family used to breed pedigrees. We had British blues, blue and white bicolours, British shorthairs, lilac points and more. I also know many of them aren't even capable of hunting, as I remember ours not being hunters at all. They were either too soft, too lazy or simply uninterested. But if you have a cat that is a hunter, then I believe you have a responsibility to prevent them from hunting birds. There are many small things you can do to achieve this: put a bell on the cat's collar, which can alert the birds to its presence; restrict outdoor access, especially during peak hunting times like dawn and dusk; and ensure that you're keeping it sufficiently stimulated, playing with fake mice or feather toys and using puzzle feeders, which can satisfy a cat's need for play and exercise without it hunting and killing birds.

In this case, I'm not sure if a domestic cat was responsible for Bobbin's disappearance, as the garden is in a remote place away from other houses and there aren't any cats in the area that I've ever seen. But it's worth considering the impact of cats on bird populations more generally. Now, as birds face so many threats because of loss of habitat, a huge decline in insects (mainly due to pesticides), and natural predators, it is more important than ever to think about where we can help. It is easy to think, 'Oh my cat only kills one or two birds a week,' but if you multiply that by the number of cats in the country, then the figures are catastrophic! Just a little effort and making small changes could make a huge difference.

When there was still no sign of him, I had to face the fact that Bobbin was not going to return. I was gutted to lose him, and not even a year after losing Bob. Bobbin was never a replacement for Bob, but he, Bobette and then Ruby certainly helped ease the pain of losing Bob, and they certainly filled a huge void.

The following Tuesday, with Bobbin still nowhere to be seen, I reluctantly decided to share the sad news with our followers on social media. The reaction to Bob going missing had been huge, so I braced myself, as I knew how much Bobbin meant to everyone too. He had battled his way into the hearts of so many who still missed Bob, with his charm and happy-go lucky ways, and we lost him way too soon. Nature is beautiful and yet so cruel at times. Of course, the comments and messages came flooding in as sorrow and disbelief once again filled my Instagram and Facebook pages. There was nothing I could do but carry on.

Ruby remained in the territory, and I would leave her mealworms and other bird food on a post in the hedge. I felt sorry for her as spring was well underway and she was now all alone. Robins are usually monogamous for the breeding season and knowing this worsened my fears about Bobbin. It was early springtime and mating season was far from over, so it was unlikely that Bobbin had abandoned his mate or left his territory, which gave more weight to the theory that he had been predated. I was also concerned about Ruby. Without a mate, she would be much more vulnerable and less able to defend her territory. I wondered what she would do next: leave to find another partner or remain on her own? Or would another male move in on Bobbin's territory and take over from him?

Within a week of Bobbin's disappearance, I noticed a lot of activity in the area from robins I didn't know. There was a lot of chasing and squabbling going on very close to Bobbin's territory and where Ruby had remained. The boys were clearly fighting it out over Ruby! In fact, they were so preoccupied that I could stand very close and they didn't seem to notice me.

After a couple of days, it became apparent that one of the robins had paired up with Ruby – I'm guessing he was the victor! It certainly wasn't Bobbin returning, because the new robin would keep his distance from me, unlike Bobbin who had always been very forthcoming and happy to interact with me. This all happened within a week of Bobbin disappearing! Bobbin and Ruby had only been together for a few months in total, as Bobbin had been with Bobette the previous year. So maybe no emotional bonds had really developed between them. When Bob lost Betty the year before, he had already been through at least one breeding season with her, and he certainly appeared to be grief-stricken: in my opinion he showed obvious signs that he was depressed or grieving. Ruby, however, seemed quite happy with her new partner, without a second thought for Bobbin. I later named the male newcomer Chip.

But this change of partner made me think even more about Bob. Was the desire to breed, the need to find a partner, the call of nature simply too strong for Bob to ignore? Is he still living his life, maybe just a field away? Not so far away, but too far to come home?

I'll probably never know the answer to that, but, after seeing how Chip moved in on Bobbin's territory, there's good reason to think that perhaps Bob did the same and found himself a new partner. Bob had always defended his territory with confidence and authority, but once Betty disappeared I watched him become downtrodden, giving up much of his territory to Bobbin and Bobette in the spring. It made perfect sense to me that he would eventually move on to find a new partner and new territory to defend, no matter how difficult it may have been for him to leave his beloved plum tree, and, I like to think, me.

Ruby was alone for no more than a week before Chip moved in on Bobbin's territory. Ruby was far less confident with me than Bobbin had been, but she battled through her uncertainties to keep some sort of relationship going. I was not going to forget about her in any case, and I continued to leave food for her in the usual places. As I passed through her territory, she started making loud repetitive calls, seemingly aimed at getting my attention, just as Bobbin used to do, although his calls were a more delicate twittering. She would do this as she awaited my return from the lake or bonfire area, excitedly calling and making her presence known as she fidgeted on a branch hanging from the hedge. As I approached, her confidence would wane, and she would back off into the safety of the hedge. She was brave, but cautious.

I had had a similar sort of relationship with

Bobette the previous year, when I got to know her as Bobbin's partner. Bobbin, as the bold, confident male, always took the lead, with the females staying back but close by. Now Bobette was with her new partner, and they were showing all the signs of being a breeding pair: Bobette fluttering her wings and screeching loudly – the call of a female robin begging her partner for food – with him willingly obliging. I haven't got to know her new partner, as he remains cautious around me, always keeping his distance. If I have any sort of interaction with Bobette, leaving food for her on the plum tree or on a post in the hedge, for example, she'll happily come close to help herself, but she is difficult to film as she is so wary, just like Ruby. Bobette's new partner is even more so, and will wait for me to back away completely before helping himself to an easy meal. This was a new experience, seeing robins I had known in some cases for a year as they began the breeding season anew in a variety of circumstances, leaving for new territory or bringing new partners into their existing one.

* * *

As spring goes on, I'm seeing less of the robins, since Bobette and Ruby are spending most of their time on their nests, incubating their eggs, and I'm much busier myself with work. The lawns are starting to grow at a rapid rate now that the weather is warming up, and weeds are growing in the flowerbeds. The work of a gardener is never done, and it's my job to keep the garden looking good all year round.

The late spring and summer period brings a host of other garden birds with different breeding patterns out into the garden. While robins stay in the UK throughout the year, repeating their cycle of meeting a mate, staking out and defending territory, nesting and raising a brood, many other birds leave the UK for a warmer climate in the winter and return home for summer. These include house martins, swallows and swifts, which all migrate from Africa. On many occasions I've taken great pleasure in watching the swallows drinking from the lake. They circle the water, sometimes in groups, then with perfect timing and great precision they swoop down and drink on the wing, opening their beaks to scoop up the water. It is quite a sight and I am in awe of their accuracy; a mistimed swoop could be fatal if they ended up in the water. It is great, too, to see them lined up on the telephone wires as they gather in numbers, readying themselves for the long migration south for the winter. I am also delighted to have seen skylarks in the field next door to where the robins live. I've watched as one shoots into the sky singing his song, seeming to go out of view as his song carries through the air – it is quite something to witness.

In Kent, we are also particularly lucky to have the possibility of seeing nightingales. Sadly, in the last 40 years, numbers of nightingales in the UK have fallen by 90 per cent, but they do still migrate from sub-Saharan Africa to the south-east of Britain in summer. I am unlikely to see one in the garden, as they generally keep to dense scrubland, but what a treat it would be to hear their famous, beautiful song.

Other favourite birds to spot during late spring and summer are green woodpeckers as they peck at the ground eating ants. The woodpecker is a nervous bird, so they are not always easy to spot – they quickly sound their alarm call and make their escape if they feel they've been seen. I also enjoy watching a particular pair of wagtails as they survey the lawn, living up to their name with their tails wagging as they run along. I am always glad to spot these birds – in the garden, on nearby buildings or swooping through the sky – but they don't behave like robins or seem to recognize specific humans, so I am less able to spot particular individuals or track their behaviours through the year as I do with the robins.

I do see the two male robins hunting for food occasionally as they provide for the females, and every now and then Bobette and Ruby will make an appearance. One morning, Ruby stood confidently close by me as she preened herself. Maybe she just needed five minutes of quiet and she knew she was safe with me. I was able to film the moment as she delicately worked her way through the orange feathers on her chest with her beak. Preening is essential to keep feathers in good condition. The bird spreads oil from her preen gland and cleans off dirt and parasites, ensuring the feathers are waterproof, provide good insulation, and are in tip-top condition for flight. It really is a privilege to witness such a moment of calm and vulnerability, especially from a female robin.

I do not know exactly where Bobette or Ruby's nests are, although I'm sure Bobette had her nest in the outbuilding again, as I saw her going in and out of it on a number of occasions. As April progressed, both females left their nests more frequently. Bobette would greet me in the mornings when I got to work. I'd park my van in the same place in front of the picket fence, which is in her and her partner's territory. Often I will arrive just before sunrise, and Bobette will make herself known by landing on the wing mirror of my van, patiently waiting for me to open the window. She'll fly away as soon as I do, though, as the noise spooks her, but she returns within seconds.

I will sit in my van drinking my coffee for ten or fifteen minutes before starting work, and Bobette will enjoy an easy breakfast as I offer her mealworms and suet pellets to help her start the day. The male robin will sometimes stand on the picket fence watching, but he never comes near, although I will throw a mealworm or two in his direction, which he hesitantly accepts. I know the robins are working hard to keep themselves in good condition and to provide for their families, so the least I can do is to offer them a boost before the day gets going.

The territories have slightly shifted as Ruby and her partner, Chip, now occupy all the mixed hedge and plum tree area, down to the compost bins. Ruby is starting to make more of an appearance these days, and will now confidently approach me hoping for an easy snack when I'm in her territory. Of course, I oblige. Unlike Bobette's partner, Chip stays close to Ruby and soon accepts me being in their territory. Before I know it, he is taking food from my hand too!

At this time of year, I try to ensure that what I give them is simply fuel for them as working parents. They need to take fresh food to their young rather than these extras, so I am sparing with my offerings, although I am sure some of the food I give them does end up going to the fledglings. I will often find myself joined by Ruby and Chip as I weed the veg garden, and they hop around by my feet as they look for any creatures that get dug up. Saa lies on the grass between the mixed hedge and the veg garden, loyally staying close, paying no attention to the robins as they bound around within inches of him. Pup, meanwhile, is more loyal to the idea of a treat from my customer, so he stays by the house, safe in the knowledge that I will return to him.

* * *

In early May, I spend most of my time working in the flowerbeds near the house in the territory of Bobette and her partner (who I never did name), so I'm seeing a lot more of them than I am of Ruby and Chip. This year, weeds have been growing at a rapid rate as the ground is warmed by the spring sunshine.

During this period, if Bobette wasn't on the nest, she would often follow me around, watching what I was doing from the handle of the wheelbarrow, or perched on my fork after I'd loosened the soil ready to weed. This is a good vantage point from which to see any critters or bugs who might have been disturbed as I made my way round the flowerbeds. It's a team effort: I do all the work, and she gets the rewards! It's taken a long time for her to trust me, and this certainly isn't a bad thing, but it's lovely that she is comfortable with me now. I find it genuinely intriguing how very different their personalities all are. One morning I watched as Bobette was calling her partner to feed her. She was standing on the edge of a large urn planter on the patio, and I knew this would be a great opportunity to film an intimate moment between a male and female robin. Her partner soon appeared and landed in front of her with a huge earthworm! I stood motionless and filmed it all on my phone. Moments like these are difficult to capture as they normally take place in sheltered areas – in the hedge or on the ground under a shrub – and they usually happen so fast that I don't have time to get my phone out my pocket so this was an opportunity, right out in the open, not to be missed.

There was a high-pitched squeak from Bobette, followed by the male passing her the worm and then flying away. First, Bobette put the worm down, readjusted it, then picked it back up and swallowed it whole. I did feel sorry for the poor worm, which was still wiggling as she swallowed it whole. The brutal side of nature was playing out before my very eyes. We often feel sympathy for the cute, fluffy animals killed by predators, but we rarely have such feelings for the less cuddly creatures of the world such as earthworms or insects.

* * *

The garden is made up of a good few acres, surrounded by fields and countryside. Looking down the garden from the back of the house, you'll see a large patio, which spans the length of the house and leads onto a large lawn. The lawn slightly falls away into the top half of the orchard, where there is rougher grassland, before a stock fence spanning the width of the garden with a gate in the middle leading to the second part of the orchard, with winding grass paths leading to the lake at the bottom.

The grass of the orchard is always cut longer than the main lawn as it is a rougher area. The fruit trees are placed sporadically, and each tree has their own large grass island planted with daffodils, which always provide amazing displays in the spring. I leave the grass islands around the trees to grow naturally throughout the year, only cutting them down in the autumn. This is great for the wildlife, and I often see voles scurrying through the long grass. It also seems to really benefit the rich insect life of the garden: damselflies from the lake often rest on the long stems of grass, making them arch over, and on

*Above* Bob perched on a birdbath in the garden

*Left* Bob in winter, with flakes of snow on his head

*Above* Bob with one of his babies, possibly Bobette

*Left* The last selfie with Bob: Tony and Bob in the garden

Family likeness:
Bobette (above) showing
her markings, which
resemble Bob's (below)

*Left* A curious baby blackbird

*Below* A male blackbird taking advantage of an easy meal in the snow

Bobbin posing in front of the poppies:
the photo that reignited Tony's love for photography

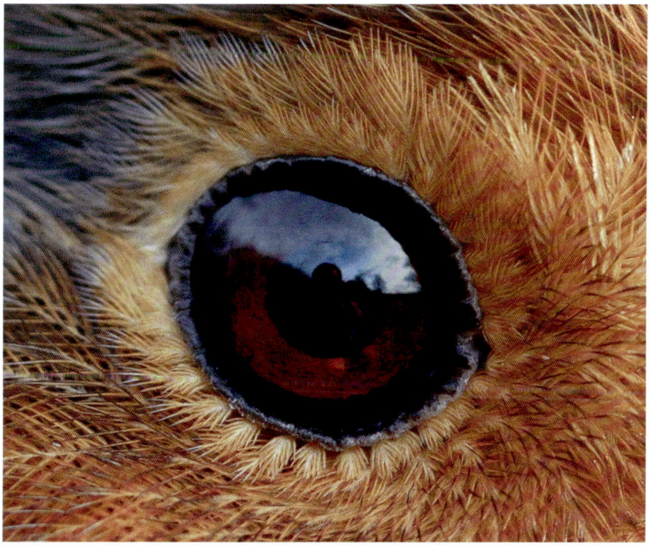

A close-up shot of Bobbin's eye

A year of hard work takes its toll as Bobette starts her annual moult

The leaves are turning as the year gets old and autumn begins

*Right* Dave the crow, the wind exposing the colour beneath his feathers

*Below* Bob the robin and Saa by the lake

*Left* Tony, Joanna and their two dogs Pup and Saa at their first home in Crowborough

*Below* Pup and Saa playfighting

dewy mornings the sun illuminates the droplets of water, revealing all the spiderwebs situated within the grass. The insects we share the garden with are an often overlooked, but absolutely crucial, element of the ecosystem. Though we may recoil at creatures such as worms or spiders, without them there would be no food for the birds, no pollination for the plants, and fewer nutrients for the soil. Insect populations are declining rapidly the world over, so it is worth doing everything we can in our own gardens to help them to thrive there. It really can be as simple as allowing the grass to grow a little longer or leaving piles of old leaves, bark or other dead plants as shelters.

The wildlife in this part of the garden can be truly spectacular, and I often see deer roaming around by the lake. When I spot them, I usually stop to observe as they casually walk the line of the hedges. I'm always fascinated to see how such a large animal can seem to blend in so well with its surroundings and can disappear in an instant when startled or threatened. I simply take pleasure in watching from a distance, doing my best to stay out of sight, knowing that any wrong move or the slightest sound could send them running. I've even seen kingfishers, although they are difficult to spot. They fly very rapidly as they circle the lake at canopy height, and despite their distinctive bright plumage you can miss them very easily!

Though I know the robins best of all, being attuned to the entire ecosystem of the garden is a wonderful way to watch a year go by. The cyclical nature of gardening has certainly helped me through some of the more difficult times in my life, as it always reminds me that change is likely to be just around the corner.

The beautiful white and lavender-coloured wisteria I so carefully pruned during the winter is now cascading from the pergola, which runs the width of the other side of the house in front of the ornamental pond. There is a laburnum tree at each end, and these are now also in full flower as their golden blooms illuminate the entrance of the pergola inviting you to walk through its golden gates.

I read somewhere that to get your wisteria to flower to its full potential, you should cut each stem back to within four buds during the winter and then cut back to two buds in early spring. I can't say that I follow this method exactly – I always cut back to two buds in winter as I simply don't have time to go over the whole pergola again in the spring – but the results are always stunning! A sweet, nostalgic smell in the air, the sound of bees buzzing as they collect pollen and nectar: it's a real feast for the senses! This has become a favourite place for Bobette to greet me now, too, even though her nest is on the other side of the house, and the laburnum and wisteria make a lovely backdrop for any photographs or films I share with my followers on social media.

It's said that if you do a job you like, you never work a day in your life, and over the years I have grown to appreciate what I do for a living more and more. Most people enjoy their garden – pottering around, making tranquil spaces, inviting the wildlife into their outdoor space. In being able to do this both at home and in my job, I get the best of both worlds. Sure, it's hard work a lot of the time, but I get to spend my days in the fresh air. And I'm able to observe the wildlife as it goes about its day, whether that's a bee collecting pollen, a bird feeding a fledgling, or the deer skipping across the fields and effortlessly jumping hedges. I'll often pause to take in the moment, silently watching as life goes on around me, and I do my best to enjoy these gardens as well as to work in them. Just as gardening reminds me that change is constant and that everything has its season, it also makes me realize how much beauty there is around us when we just take the time to notice. Attuning my senses to appreciate the little things is something I try to apply to the rest of my life, too, being grateful for pleasures like a cup of coffee in the morning, and small acts of love from my partner, friends or family.

* * *

I hadn't forgotten about Ruby or Chip, of course, and would make several trips through their territory throughout the day. I had to pass the plum tree there whenever I needed to empty the wheelbarrow either onto the bonfire or into the compost bins. Robins have excellent eyesight so they can see me coming a mile off. If they want an easy meal, or even just want to let me know they're still around, they will make themselves known as I approach, either with twittering sounds or chirping, or even by standing in complete silence but in plain sight at eye level. They'll often do this from the branch of the plum tree where I first met Bob. It has become the heart of the garden for me, where everything began, where blossoms continue to bloom every spring, and where new generations of robins enjoy perching and getting to know me.

# Chapter Five

# True Friendship

June arrives and we are suddenly halfway through the year. Both pairs of robins have successfully raised a brood of young. I did see the babies, but neither of the parents introduced them to me – I simply observed from a distance as Mum and Dad fed the demanding fledglings! Bobette and Chip have since remained in their respective territories, but I don't know where Ruby has gone, where Bobette's partner went, or why either of them left so early. Robins will often have more than one brood, with the male robins taking care of the first fledglings while the females get to work on a new nest, so nesting activity often extends well into June or July before the adults start moulting. But whatever the reason for their departure, life in the garden continues, and the other robins keep up their daily antics. It's the season for lavender and there is now a lot of it in the garden. There is something so nostalgic about lavender. Maybe it's the smell or the striking blue-purple sea of flowers attracting the bees and butterflies. It has the real feel-good factor of summer, and I just love it!

In some of the flowerbeds there are ornamental posts with lights embedded in them, and they offer a great perch for a curious robin. One of the wooden posts is positioned among the flowering lavender and, with Bobette so willing to land on it, I couldn't pass up a photo opportunity. As an experienced photographer for over ten years, I always take photos in manual mode, which means that I choose all the settings myself: shutter speed, ISO and aperture. I'm in full control of the camera and I also only shoot in Raw format.

With my camera at the ready, I waited by the post knowing that Bobette was likely to appear to see what I was up to – she follows me around so much now that this would not be unusual for her. Before I knew it, and as predicted, there she was, perched on the post among the lavender, so I checked my settings on the camera and took her photo. I took several as she calmly looked on, some as portraits and others as landscapes. This is not just for variety, but also because photos shared on social media pages work better in portrait format, as most people view their social media on their phones. It comes as part of the territory now to always consider what is most helpful to my followers as they tell me how much they love these photos!

I also try to make physical versions of my photos, to really display the high-quality pictures in their original formats. Since 2015, the first full year of my learning photography, I have had a calendar made for my customers using images from that year, and I continue to do so to this day. Joanna, my wife, built a website for us to sell the products, and it is most humbling when we sell a calendar or cards, knowing that my photography is liked enough for people to buy it, and, even more impressively, for them to gift it to someone else. It is always a thrilling feeling. I can state with confidence that if it wasn't for my wife then none of this would be happening at all. There is no way that I could build or maintain the website – and the problems that occur when printing are endless! We operate as a team, and this affords me the time to concentrate on my filming, photography, and keeping our followers up to date on social media, as well as doing my job. Joanna really is one in a million and I'm so lucky to have her in my life. We have been together for over twenty years, always working in partnership and trying to do what is best for one another. Of course, there have been highs and lows over the years, just like in any relationship, but we navigate the rough with the smooth. Every challenge and every obstacle we have overcome makes us stronger, and there have certainly been many!

* * *

I've known Bobette since December 2022, so over a year and a half at this point, but it's only now that she's really starting to accept me. It is hard to explain, but it's the feeling of true friendship rather than something transactional. I have a handful of people in my life I consider to be true friends. I can act silly around them, I can be serious, but they always feel like home, wherever we are. They are my people, and however distant from me, or however much time we've spent apart, the bond remains the same.

I certainly feel that I had this bond with Bob. He didn't just see me as someone who gave him a mealworm whenever he wanted one. He saw me as a friend. Of course, some people will say 'animals or wild animals don't or can't think like that; it's just cupboard love.' But I beg to differ. I've had animals around me all my life, cats and dogs, for instance, and I certainly consider them to be my friends and family and not merely pets. And the same goes for the pets of other people I know.

Here's one example. The people in the house opposite where I work have a dog called Fred, whom I've known since he was a puppy, though only really in passing. If he's with his owner I'll say hello to him, or if he's at the gate I'll pay him lots of attention. Fred must be seven or eight years old now and I have never given him a treat as his owners don't like people feeding their dog, which is completely understandable. I've never spent long periods of time with Fred, but if he sees me outside his gate, his head will go down as if he's trying to hide a big smile, his tail will wag, and he will whine with excitement as he approaches me. I'll make a fuss of him for no more than a minute and then he'll be off, back into his garden. Fred clearly sees me as a friend.

These bonds certainly develop, whether with a domesticated or a wild animal. I vividly remember the last month or two when Bob was around; his world had shrunk after losing his partner and then he'd surrendered his territory to Bobbin and Bobette. The time he spent with me felt so much more than him just following me around. I watched him watching me, as if he was really taking in every moment we had together: it was as if he was preparing himself to be able to leave his true friend. I knew things were changing, and deep down I knew that I'd turn up one day and he would be gone. But Bob trusted me completely, and as he stood there on the ground, looking so tiny, as if he was frozen or in a trance watching me, I would slowly approach him and gently stroke his orange breast. I could hardly feel him he was so soft and light, so I was careful not to push him over, but he didn't flinch or back away at all. He really seemed to welcome the comforting touch and interaction of his dear friend; that was such a powerful moment for me and, I like to think, for him too.

* * *

I consider Bobette to be a quiet, observant kind of character. She's fiercely independent, but if she accepts you into her world she will be the most loyal friend. I hadn't seen Bobette's partner all month, but I did see her feeding her fledglings and I was even able to film it on one or two occasions. This was great to witness because I'd never seen Betty, Bob's partner, feeding their fledglings, only Bob himself doing so, which meant I was getting a greater insight into the life of a female robin now, and how hard they too work to feed their young. In fact it seemed as if Bobette was the only one feeding her fledglings now!

Chip's work as a parent appeared to be over for the year as he had started his annual moult. It seemed to be happening early – I'd usually observe Bob moulting in the month of August. Chip has abandoned his territory and moved to the compost bins, just as Bobbin had done the year before. I could also see that he'd lost his tail, so flying was a little more difficult. I make life a little easier for him by leaving small piles of mealworms and food on the compost bin posts, so he doesn't have to venture too far for food. There is still no sign of Ruby.

Bobette is showing no signs of moulting yet and she has slightly shifted her territory too. She has now taken over Chip's old patch of the mixed hedge and the plum tree and is still occupying most of the garden as she continues to feed her young. I have noticed another robin near the house and as there appears to be no conflict, I'm confident that this one is Bobette's partner, although I have no idea where he has been for the past month or why I haven't seen him. I guess it isn't too difficult for a little robin to remain out of sight if he wants to keep a low profile.

By mid-July, however, Bobette has also begun her annual moult. I can see the white feathers below the orange of her breast starting to thin as her older feathers fall out, slowly being replaced by new ones.

One hot, sunny day, I was deadheading the roses, which involved pruning the spent flowers, cutting just above a node or new shoot to encourage fresh flowering. It's a never-ending job during the summer months: all the flowerbeds have a rose or two in them and they are very well established and covered in blooms.

I never wear gardening gloves when I'm deadheading or pruning roses, and there is a good reason for this. I find that the thorns get snagged on my gloves and I end up getting more thorns in me than if I *don't* wear gloves, so I've just learned to handle the roses with my bare hands and to take care when working with them. I prune the spent flowers back to a new bud, always cutting at an angle to prevent any rainwater from sitting on the fresh cut as it can cause disease or rot. We always have amazing displays of beautiful iceberg white roses, pink roses, and a large maigold next to the house. The pergola has a blend of climbing roses mixed in with the wisteria and of course we have a couple of red roses, with their velvety-looking petals. The garden is a real picture of beauty at this time of the year.

There are large ornamental yew trees in the flowerbeds, too, some over 10 feet tall! These are kept tightly trimmed into cone shapes, as they start off wide at the base, getting thinner as they form into a point at the top. There are seven of these trees situated in the flowerbeds along one side of the garden, and they offer great shelter and protection for any small bird as they can get deep inside the dense, tightly compact foliage to escape harsh weather or to avoid predators.

I was very much in Bobette's territory when pruning the roses, and, with her babies now fledged and gone, it was time for her to concentrate on herself. She followed me about that day, but it wasn't because she wanted food from me, even though I did of course offer her a mealworm or two. There was plenty of natural food in the form of insects, which were everywhere! I realized she had stuck close by me for a different reason when she lay down next to me in the sun, with her wings spread out on the ground as if she was sunbathing. When I'd seen other robins do this I'd been a little unnerved to begin with: my first thought, when Bob did it, was that there must be something wrong. But I soon realized that it was a perfectly normal behaviour on sunny days, and something that is actively good for a bird's health. It is thought that robins and other garden birds sunbathe in order to keep their feathers healthy. Bird feathers are kept strong and flexible by preen oil, which is secreted from a gland near the base of the tail. Sunlight and warmth helps to spread this oil around the bird's body and feathers, ensuring that they are kept moisturized. The sunlight may also help to remove any parasites or lice in the feathers, with the spread of preen oil making it easier for the birds to dislodge them with their beaks, or because the heat from the sun and UV rays kill the parasites directly. Moreover, she is moulting. This is an uncomfortable process, and must be very itchy as the new feathers push their way through, dislodging the old ones. Perhaps the sunlight brings some relief. Bobette was probably using me to be able to sunbathe safely since a predator would be unlikely to attack her when so close to me. They're clever little birds, these robins! Water is also very important, not only for hydration in hot weather but also for the maintenance of their feathers, so I always make sure that the birdbath by the plum tree and the tray beneath the mixed hedge is full. It was lovely to know that Bobette trusted me, especially at a time when she was vulnerable.

By the end of July, Bobette had lost her tail due to moulting. She was keeping a low profile, sticking close to the plum tree and mixed hedge, and Chip was doing the same, but by the compost bins. I'd place mealworms on the posts of the bins for Chip and on a log ring under the mixed hedge for Bobette, and they'd make themselves known as they helped themselves to an easy meal. There is plenty of natural food about for them to eat, but leaving the safety of the hedge without a tail or full body of feathers to hunt for food leaves the birds open to attack, so I like to help make their day a little easier if I can.

My thoughts were never far away from Bob, or from any of the robins I've known over the years, and I continued sharing photos and videos of Bob on my social media pages as I know how much our followers love to see him. Even though he'd been gone for over a year, his presence was still strong – he was still commanding the limelight! And now, the finishing touches were being done to his book, too, which was almost ready for publication day in October.

# Chapter Six

# Bob in Print

I was of the belief that all of Bobette's fledglings had moved on, especially as Bobette was now well into her moult, but I was wrong. At least one or two of them were still around, and Bobette continued to care for them. One of the babies was standing on a branch of the plum tree, with brown plumage on its back, a speckled breast where the orange would soon be, and lighter colouring underneath. It watched me for a moment and then nervously retreated to the safety of the hedge. I knew from watching Bob and his predecessors that the male as well as the female will feed the fledglings during the breeding season, the pair of them working as a team to maximize the number of broods: with the male doing the feeding, the female can concentrate on the next batch of eggs. The mortality rate of robins is very high, especially in the first 12 to 18 months, so it makes sense to have as many babies as possible. I saw Bob's partner,

Betty, and of course Bobette, raising her young with Bobbin the previous year, but I had a more trusting relationship with the male robins, and I couldn't get as close to the females.

Despite what I had seen with the other pairs of robins, I hadn't seen Bobette's new partner feeding any fledglings since June, and I hadn't seen him near Bobette at all since then. Maybe, after multiple broods, the females finish the job of raising the last batch of young, or maybe Bobette and her partner's relationship just worked slightly different to Bob and Betty's. I really don't know – but it's great to witness and learn new things! It is always fascinating to see how the individual robins and pairings have their own personalities and behaviours that don't always match up with the research or what you can read about robins. That's another thing I love about being a gardener: working outdoors, and having the time to get to know each of the birds, there's always more to learn.

It was around this time that I noticed Bobette's behaviour change around me. Our regular meeting place was the ringed log that was on the other side of the plum tree and mixed hedge, tucked up in a corner between the hedge and a low fence. I'd sit beside the log as she'd make her way towards me, hopping from branch to branch within the mixed hedge until she reached me. When she landed on the log, she would stand on one leg, and I'd offer her a mealworm. She'd take it from me standing on two legs, but then immediately go back to standing on just one. Bob would sometimes do this too, and after doing some research, I learned that this can be a sign that a bird is either cold or they are comfortable in your presence and accept you. It certainly wasn't cold in August, so she must've been accepting me! I remember feeling so pleased that she was allowing me a little more into her world with every passing day.

As the days get shorter and the summer slowly

begins to yield to autumn, I often watch the sunrise with Bobette as she stands on the branch of the plum tree, where I so often watched the start of a new day, with Bob, Pup and Saa always close by. There's a slight chill in the misty air but the sun soon burns through to warm the land, a reminder of what was, and what is to come. I feel a great sense of nostalgia as we see in the new day. As I look over to Bobette, I think of Bob and all the people and animals I've known in my life. For me, the sunrise is a moment to reflect on and remember the past but to also look forward to the future. Every sunrise means the start of a new day that could bring anything. Bobette is still going through her moult, and she looks a little moth-eaten as she's losing the feathers around her face. But the worst is over and she'll soon have a full body of new feathers, ready to take on the winter to come. Chip is still living by the compost bins, and he's looking in fine shape. His moult is over – he started before Bobette, so he had a little head start. I still haven't seen Ruby, but she has probably established her own territory nearby.

Bobette still meets me by the ringed log, our usual meeting place. But her movements haven't gone unnoticed by other birds in the garden. A lone great tit has started following her: I can see it as she makes her way through the hedge to me. It doesn't join her on the log, but remains close by in the safety of the hedge. I always leave a small pile of mealworms on the log for Bobette, so the great tit appears to have taken note of this and helps itself to an easy meal after I've gone.

Great tits, like many other garden birds, follow similar breeding and nesting patterns to robins and, also like robins, they rarely migrate to other countries during winter. They are very common in the UK, and I had often heard them in the garden, recognizable by their distinctive call, which many have identified as sounding like 'Teacher Teacher'! I once had the pleasure of hearing this call first-hand and at very close quarters. As I was interacting with one of the robins, a great tit landed on the branch of the tree just above my head and sounded the call, making me jump – it was very loud and right in my ear! I remember that Bob used to like landing next to me without me noticing and then he'd suddenly sing in my ear – as charming as it is, it can be quite startling if you're not expecting it. The great tit was a lovely reminder of the seemingly mischievous things Bob used to get up to, like making me jump with his beautiful melodic songs.

* * *

The day Bob's book arrived was surreal. It was such a strange feeling to hold it in my hands: a mixture of pride; sadness, as I knew Bob wouldn't get to see it; and a little bit of disbelief that I had actually written a book for the world to read! I thought it would be a nice idea to show the book to Bobette: after all, I do believe that she is Bob's daughter.

I placed the book standing up on the ringed log and, although hesitant at first, Bobette flew from the hedge and landed right on it! I knew immediately that this would make a great photo or video for my socials: Bob on the cover, with Bobette standing on top of him – what a great image! I managed to take a few photos with my phone, and filmed a couple of videos of her with the book. This was the sort of thing I'd hoped to do with Bobbin before he disappeared, but sadly that wasn't to be.

The book had been announced to all our followers, and I felt an enormous amount of pride and then self-doubt as the realization hit me of what this meant. What if nobody wants the book? What if people don't like it and it doesn't live up to expectation? It's not as if I've written a fictional novel. This is the true story of my life and my friendship with Bob. How can such a true story be judged by a reader? Yet of course that is exactly what will happen. My life is now out there, ready for a star rating, and to be critiqued by anyone who reads my story. It's not as if I'm a well-known public figure or a celebrity living in the spotlight. I am just a guy who shares photos and videos of robins from a garden where I work; I have no ambition or desire to be in the public eye. The robins are all I intended to share – they were to be the stars. But sometimes life unfolds unexpectedly and it becomes difficult to avoid being seen too. I'd put so much time and effort into writing Bob's story and wanting to do him proud that I really hadn't considered the potential negative reactions that could come my way, so the excitement was certainly mixed with anxiety. But there was no way back now.

With the anticipation of Bob's book came requests from the media to do interviews. Yes, I have done TV and radio interviews about Bob in the past, and no, I didn't enjoy them, although the more I did, the more relaxed I became. I love sharing the robins, but I still have no interest in being the focus of attention myself, although it's becoming difficult to avoid.

BBC South East requested an interview, and asked if they could come to where Bob lived and see me with the robins. I had to agree of course, because I wanted the book to do well, and I knew that many people would see it on the news. I suggested early morning, because there was more chance they would see Bobette at that time rather than later in the day. To me, the robins do just seem a little more sociable in the morning. I met the reporter, Hannah, at the garden at 7am. It was a cold and frosty morning, so there was a good chance she would get to see Bobette. I had no idea, however, how Bobette would react to the presence of someone she didn't know: if she was anything like Bob, then she would stay out of sight. Bob really was a one-man robin!

But Hannah had a very relaxed manner about her, and she made me feel at ease from the moment we met. She had a dry wit, which normally indicates to me that someone is easy-going. She was also smart because she rigged me up with a microphone right away and started recording before the interview had started. She asked me questions continuously as she set up her camera and got herself ready for the interview proper: 'How long did you know Bob? It must be great knowing such a special bird. What's it like having a book out?' When the interview started, I was – I must be honest – all over the place! I know that my mind can shut down sometimes, and I can be very blunt and matter of fact with one-word answers, and that is pretty much what happened!

Hannah was asking me questions that most people would answer and expand on, but I was stuck in one-word-answer mode, and the more I tried to snap out of it the worse I got! Hannah picked up on this and stopped the interview, asking instead if we could try to find Bobette. Of course, I was more than happy to do that, but she kept recording, and continued to ask me all the relevant interview questions. But because I was now relaxed and back in my comfort zone, I answered everything and elaborated with ease. I knew I was rubbish that day, but because of Hannah's professionalism, what was shown on the telly and the way the interview came out was so much better than the reality, and I am so grateful to her for that. I also did a few radio interviews. Most of these were only two or three minutes long, with the hosts asking me the same questions, and to be honest I did find them a bit difficult. Talking about Bob, when losing him still felt very painful, really brought everything to the surface. It was an odd feeling speaking to people who hadn't really read the book, especially when they were so enthusiastic and excited but didn't know me or Bob, about something that was so personal and had had such a big impact on my life.

The best interview was with Bernie Keith of BBC Radio Northampton. It certainly helped that he had read the book and also had an interest in robins, so the conversation flowed naturally and with ease because of this common ground; he wasn't simply trying to fill a three-minute time slot. I have certainly learned the difference between a genuine interview and one that's just filling a gap, and I do my best to avoid the gap fillers now.

* * *

The book was published and officially out in the world. I started it when Bob was still with me, but had to finish it without him. It was very bittersweet for me: it was wonderful to be able to write a book about my dear friend, but the memories and emotions were still very raw, and it was taxing to write. I felt guilty knowing his book would be available for everyone to read, but with Bob himself missing from my side. It took hours of work, and digging up memories, and was a labour of love. Yet there was a lot of sorrow, knowing that he will never see it. Yes, Bob is a robin, but he was certainly my friend, and a friend to all our followers on social media, especially those who followed our story during the dark years of Covid. I miss him dearly, and our followers do too. The book has become more than just a book. It is now his legacy, and a story to outlive me, and to live on for as long as it's on someone's bookshelf.

After the book was out I shared a song I wrote about Bob with my followers on social media. It was heartfelt and I knew it would be especially emotional for my followers who knew and loved him. The song had over 42,000 views, nearly 8,000 likes and over 220 comments on Instagram. Here are some of the comments: 'This song is so beautiful, it made me feel quite emotional'; 'Beautiful song for beautiful Bob'; 'Oh Tony, that made me cry'; 'Wonderful tribute'.

I wrote Bob's song during the summer as I cut the grass at work. I find that my thoughts can take me all over the place when I'm mowing but it's a great time for reflection too. The lyrics kept popping into my head, but I couldn't write them down, so when I emptied the mower, I sent the lyrics as a bunch of messages to my wife on my phone, doing my best to remember them as I wrote them. She must've wondered what on earth I was on about as she received note after random note. But the words just kept coming as I remembered Bob, my dear feathered friend. I didn't see them as lyrics at the time, more as nice memories or little poems, but I knew I had to write them down, and later on I transferred them into a little black notebook. But it was only with the help of an old friend, Ashley, that it became a song.

I was a smoker for 13 years. Then one day, I bought myself a pouch of tobacco, rolled a cigarette, and didn't smoke it. That same morning, I popped round to see one of my best and oldest friends, Ashley. I've always known Ash, as I call him, to play the guitar. He had not long bought himself a new acoustic, so seeing two guitars side by side, I asked him if he would show me how to play. Pressing the strings with my fingers was so painful at first, I remember thinking, 'how on earth do people play these things! And for FUN!'

He had some songs printed out with the chords above the lyrics, and he gave me some of the ones with the simpler chords to help get me started. I remember 'Caravan of Love' by the Housemartins, 'Only You' by Yazoo, and 'Runaway Train' by Soul Asylum. Ash let me borrow his spare guitar and it wasn't long before music and playing the guitar became the new vice that helped me quit smoking. It wasn't easy, but I am so glad I persevered! I can be very stubborn at times, and my stubbornness proved a great ally when it came to quitting smoking and learning the guitar. I owe it to the patience of a great friend, who took the time to help me learn, as well as perseverance and willpower.

I never became a great musician, but I never smoked again either. I kept the rolled cigarette and tobacco on my person for around a year after I stopped smoking: I dared myself not to smoke it, and over time the will to not smoke became stronger than the urge to smoke. I then gave the cigarette and tobacco to Ash, and he still has it now, over 13 years on.

I'd totally forgotten about my little black book and what I'd written in it during the summer until I was talking to Ash one evening, and the subject of Christmas songs came up, and he said that he'd 'always wanted to write one'. Then I remembered the book! That evening, I looked through it and thought 'I'm going to put some music to these words'. I picked up my guitar and started playing chords, putting the song together in less than an hour. I was excited about what I'd created, and sent the lyrics and chords to Ash. He recorded himself playing the ukulele and singing my song and then sent it to me. When I heard it, it sent shivers down my spine. He played it exactly how I intended and it was so strange to hear my song being played, especially as he's a better musician and singer than I am! We both played around with it for a couple of weeks, changing some of the lyrics, with Ash adding some of his own. When we finally got together, I went to his house with my guitar, and we recorded the version that is on my socials. It took us a couple of hours to do, using a microphone attached to my phone, with me playing the guitar, Ash playing the ukulele and singing.

*A golden November morning you gave me a glance*
*Sitting in the tree on your favourite branch*
*Singing your song for all to hear*
*You didn't know I heard you so clear*

*When the world went dark you were the light*
*You were the spark that shone so bright,*
*When I think back to how it could've been,*
*It's clear my friend you saved me*

*Your picture I was happy to take*
*A friend in you I didn't need to make*
*A hundred many times it happened I'm sure*
*I'd lost my friends the years before*

*When the world went dark you were the light*
*You were the spark that shone so bright,*
*When I think back to how it could've been*
*It's clear my friend you saved me*

*Winter was coming I know for sure*
*You'd be around for a few months or more*
*You made me laugh, never made me cry*
*Until that day when you said goodbye*

*When the world went dark you were the light*
*You were the spark that shone so bright,*
*When I think back to how it could've been*
*It's clear my friend you saved me,*
*It's clear my friend you saved me*

* * *

It was at this point that I finally accepted that Bob wasn't coming back. There was a part of me that kept hoping for his return but it became clear to me that I had to say goodbye, and the song was my way of doing that. Many of us who have lost someone will know that feeling of expecting to see that person again. You expect them to walk into a room or be at the other end of the phone. But slowly over time it becomes real that they are gone. This is where gardening can become a lifeline for us. The longer you spend in the garden, the more you see the seasons come and go. You learn that while it will be different when spring turns to summer, summer to autumn or autumn to winter, spring will come back round again the next year. When you notice snowdrops or crocuses dying back in spring, you know they will make their way back through the soil at the end of the next winter, promising you that lighter days are ahead. When cherry blossom blooms in April, you know it will only be for a few fleeting weeks, and that is part of what makes it so beautiful. In short, there is a comfort in knowing that life keeps going. And that's what kept me at the garden.

## Chapter Seven

# The Gift of Gardening

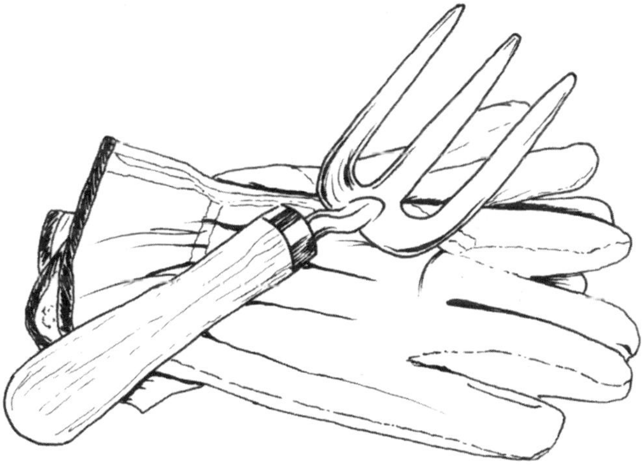

From a young age I wanted to work as a gardener, but oddly it wasn't because I had any real interest in gardening. I knew that further study wasn't my thing, and I also knew that I didn't want to be working indoors all my life, so gardening was the best prospect for me. I loved the outdoors and I knew I could earn a good living from doing it, and I quite liked the idea of being my own boss. My indifferent attitude towards gardening changed when we bought our own property with a garden. But it was a long journey to get there.

My wife and I had lived in unpleasant circumstances for five years, renting a small flat just outside my home town of Edenbridge. One day, I was stuck at home feeling sorry for myself with the flu. The damp on the walls and the cold during the winter were so bad that I decided it was time we moved out. I'd had enough of the conditions we were living in.

While Joanna was at work, and I was at home trying to recover, I called the estate agents in Edenbridge. I asked if there were any properties available to rent in the local area, and the agent said there were, but that we couldn't afford the rent for them as we needed to earn a certain amount to be considered. I felt completely deflated and trapped. I didn't know what else we could do! We were also on the council list, but it was difficult to get a council property, and we were simply getting nowhere with them.

So we were stuck between a rock and a hard place. The flat we were renting had recently been deemed a 'Grade A health hazard' because of the damp and mould. But the council wouldn't house us and the estate agent wouldn't consider us for different rental properties because we weren't earning enough, despite the fact that we were both working full-time. What other option was there for us?

What the estate agent said next really surprised

me. 'Have you considered buying a property?', she said. Of course, everyone would love to buy their own home, and we were no exception. But we never thought it possible. I'm from a council estate background, and it had become normal for me to believe that owning your own home was out of reach for us. I genuinely thought that if you owned your own property then you were doing very well for yourself, and that I was destined to never experience such a thing in my life. How wrong I was.

My wife and I had always been careful with our money. Spearheaded by my wife, we lived a very frugal lifestyle, spending what we needed and saving whatever we could. The estate agent gave me the number of a financial adviser based in East Grinstead, a town not too far from Edenbridge, so I called and explained our situation. I even remember the name of the person who agreed to meet us and discuss our options. David was such a nice person. He was really helpful and treated us with nothing but respect: it was such a positive experience for both my wife and me! He crunched the numbers, took our savings into account, and declared that we had enough money for a deposit for a one-bedroom flat in the area.

You can imagine the feeling – going from not knowing where to turn, or what to do, to suddenly being told that we could be homeowners! Of course, we immediately got looking for our first proper home, and we viewed many. And then I found a two-bed maisonette in Crowborough. My wife didn't really like it, but I was sold! The property needed everything doing, but I convinced her that it would be a good move because, for the same money, we'd be leapfrogging from buying a one-bed flat to a two-bed with a private garden!

I vividly remember our first night in our new home, in June 2011. I lay on the bed on our first night. We had no curtains on the windows, and shadows thrown up by the streetlamps moved around the room as cars passed by. There were unfamiliar noises from the unfamiliar town, and an overwhelming feeling of self-doubt and dread. We had, after all, just taken on the biggest debt of our lives and now we had no money left at all. But it was the best thing we have ever done.

We continued to live the frugal lifestyle we'd become so accustomed to while renting, and saved hard in order to do the work on the property that it so desperately needed. We also did a lot of this ourselves, removing the old kitchen and stripping away old wallpaper. I chased out the walls so that my friend Rob, an electrician, could wire new plugs in the rooms, all of which had had only one plug in them! It was real dirty work, with dust everywhere, and we had to live in it. But we knew it would all be worth it. We had a new boiler, new bathroom and new kitchen, and all the walls were plastered by my childhood friend, Mike. He and Rob both did a great job. It took us six years to complete our home, but it was well worth the upheaval.

In 2019 we decided to move. We'd worked hard, saved, and it now became apparent that we could afford to buy a bigger place. I had reservations at first, mostly because of all the work we'd put in. I knew every inch of that place as I had done all the decorating, but I'm not sure if it was love or resentment that made me hesitant about moving. I knew it had served its purpose, though, and that we had created a way to get to where we wanted to be.

We moved into our new home in September 2019: a three-bedroom end-of-terrace, with a drive and a detached garage that went alongside the house, separated by a path accessing the garden from the front. Our living room had a patio door that led out onto a raised patio area and then stepped down onto a small lawn. Our new garden wasn't very big but it was ours. To the right was a large, raised pond, with a raised area leading to the back fence, and to the left along the back of the fence was a slightly elevated flowerbed full of ground elder and a very unhealthy conifer hedge that ran the length of the garden down the left-hand side.

It all seemed fine at first, until I really looked. The pond was leaking, and when I investigated it became apparent that it was beyond repair. Everything needed fixing or redoing so I completely re-landscaped the garden soon after moving in. I dismantled the pond, and kept all the bricks and slabs used to build it. Joanna and I took out the unhealthy conifer hedge, and my dad helped me put up a 6-foot fence to secure the garden, especially important for the safety of my dogs when they're out there. I levelled the garden as best I could, meticulously going through the soil where the ground elder was to be sure that every bit of it, down to the last tiny piece of root, was gone. That stuff is a weed I really don't want because it is a nightmare to get rid of. Luckily, I'm experienced enough to know how to take my time to be sure of it, and I'm pleased to say I achieved my goal. I haven't seen any in my garden since.

With the garden now levelled, I put a pond in the far corner on the left-hand side (if looking from the house), and I planted an acer tree on the left so that it would hang over the water. In the summer the back of the pond is filled by a perennial plant that has medium-sized yellow flowers and grows as tall as the fence. I called this area 'sunshine corner', and it looks stunning! To the right of the pond is a black elder tree in a flowerbed that runs the length of the fence. There is a raised bed running down the right side of the garden, which I made using the paving slabs I'd saved to retain the soil. In the raised bed are climbing roses, which help hide the fence. I also made a flowerbed in front of the patio, which I have turned into a rose garden. The left-hand side of the garden from the pond is a flowerbed running along the fence, a vegetable garden I made by using old railway sleepers, and then the garden drops down another level, a step or two leading to the side of the house. Here there is another patio area created using recycled slabs, as well as the garage, which runs parallel with the house and is separated by a path leading to the front gate. We also have a small lawn and flowerbed at the front of the house. When we moved in there were three sheds that were in very poor condition, so I dismantled them and saved all the wood I thought could be used in the future. We had a couple of climbing roses, shrub roses, black elder tree and a few plants, but not many, so the garden needed planting!

I loved the idea of attracting birds to our garden of course, so I wanted to make it as friendly as possible for all wildlife. We planted a cherry blossom we bought ourselves as a Valentine's Day gift. I can't say that I have ever been the romantic type, or the sort of person who spends lots of money on things to show my wife how much I love her. There are a few reasons for this. Firstly, we both grew up with little money, so the money we do have is hard-earned and we carefully prioritize what we spend it on. And secondly, gifts are just not that important to us. We have a great relationship, one of equality and mutual respect, and we have always shown this in other ways. But, on Valentine's Day 2020, after I'd levelled the lawn, we did buy a tree to mark the occasion: a cherry blossom that we chose together, and that had meaning for us both.

I don't think either of us has bought the other a Valentine's gift since, but this tree lives on, providing sustenance for animals in our garden and becoming our first feeding station for the birds. The tree flowers beautifully in the spring with delicate pink blossoms that are always covered in bees and, with the bird feeders hanging from the branches, we have many a garden visitor.

All the smaller birds congregate in the trees before feasting from the bird feeders. We have an army of bickering sparrows, and they are entertaining to watch as they like having dust baths in the veg garden on hot summer days. We also have great tits, blue tits, coal tits, blackbirds and, of course, a robin or two! The pond serves the birds and other animals well too – it is a great way to attract wildlife to your garden. With rocks running round the edge and a two-slab waterfall, it is easily accessible for any bird or local wildlife that needs a drink. I'm really not choosy about which birds visit our garden, whether songbird, woodpigeon, jackdaw or magpie. They're all beautiful in their own way, and all welcome.

I also built a brick plinth with a paving slab on top, which I placed on the patio for the less nimble birds to feed from, such as the woodpigeons. I do find the woodpigeons amusing as they try pecking at the other birds in their effort to dominate the feeding station but are mostly ignored. I once watched one taking a bath in the pond's waterfall. It sat on the lowest slab, lifted its wing to allow the water to flow over it and then turned around to do the other side. How can you not smile at that?

I was keen to see what was visiting our garden at night, so I set up a trail camera. When I looked at the footage I discovered that we had a family of foxes visiting nearly every night – mum, cubs and even the dog fox. I know this because I saw him cock his leg against my plants, and was easily identifiable because he had a floppy ear and a bent tail. I guess he'd been in an accident at some time in his life.

The fox would visit during the day, and I'd often see him walking along the top of the fence, which was 6 feet high. But he had no trouble climbing it. I saw him scale the fence on many occasions: he'd make a run-up, jump halfway up, grip the fence with his paws for a second propulsion, and then he'd be on the top, just like a cat! On one occasion, I saw him when I was looking out the patio door window, so I went and got a Bonio, one of my dogs' favourite treats! As I opened the patio door the fox retreated and hid round the back of the pond, which has dense foliage, so easy for a fox to hide in. I didn't realize at the time that there was a hole in the bottom of the fence, behind the pond, so he could easily make his escape. As I didn't want to spook him by getting too close, I left the Bonio on the lawn and retreated into the house and waited. It only took a minute or two for him to reappear. I watched him approach the biscuit cautiously, gently pick it up, and then scale the fence, making off with his prize. I felt pleased knowing he'd had an easy snack. I love foxes and always have, especially after having had a close relationship with one I named Vixen a few years prior to this. But her story is in Bob's book.

Of an evening, I left a small pile of dog kibble out for the fox family, just to help them get by. What I didn't anticipate was how the dog fox would respond to being given a Bonio that day. In the afternoon the sun shines directly through the patio doors into my living room, so we have large curtains to reduce the heat and glare, especially during the summer. The day after giving the fox his treat, I was sitting on the sofa with the curtains drawn when I heard something scratching at the patio door. It was unexpected so made me jump – it was also quite loud and very deliberate! I pulled the curtain open and there was the dog fox with his floppy ear and bent tail looking at me. He approached and started scratching at the glass again as I stood looking back at him. I couldn't believe it – he was asking for another Bonio! I went and got it for him, and as I opened the patio door he retreated to the lawn. I put the biscuit on the patio and went back into the house and closed the door. This went on nearly every day for a month or so, and if I wasn't quick enough, he'd start chewing the spout of the watering can on the patio as if to say, 'hurry up, I want my treat!' That fox had me well and truly wrapped around his paw! I didn't mind though. I loved seeing him, and he was more than welcome in my garden. But

I was certainly amazed at how quickly he learned and how bold he was, especially when it came to getting his treat!

Sadly, this didn't last for long. For whatever reason, one day he just never came back. I don't know what happened to him. Perhaps he found food from another home, or he could have been hit by a car or pushed out by another dog fox. I'm not sure. I did see another dog fox in my garden so that may be why the first one stopped visiting. I know this because I watched this new fox cock his leg against one of my plants just as his predecessor did. It was a shame as I had enjoyed his daily visits, even if he was a little destructive when I took too long fetching his treat. I missed him, but that is the price for getting to know wild animals: if they stop visiting, you rarely get closure about what's happened to them. I knew this too well with Bob.

Foxes are often taken for granted in the UK, especially in cities where people even regard them as something of a nuisance. But when you take the time to actually look at them, they are truly beautiful creatures, with their red fur, bright eyes and spectacularly bushy tails. They are also highly adaptable, intelligent – some might say cunning – and, in order to survive, very good at making the best of whatever environment they find themselves in. That's probably why the fox in my garden kept coming back. He realized very quickly that he could get an easy meal and didn't waste the opportunity. I loved observing his behaviour and watching his movements in the garden. It was yet another experience that reminded me of how much excitement and beauty there is in the natural world when you start looking at creatures with fresh eyes – even and especially if you see them every day.

Another garden visitor that was more difficult to see was a badger that came nearly every night. Sometimes I would see it before it got dark, but mostly I'd catch it on my trail cam. We live in a cul-de-sac, so it was particularly unusual, and delightful, to have such a visitor. Badgers are very nervous, shy creatures, who are sensitive even to the scent of humans: they're likely to stay in their setts if they can smell us, let alone see us. Seeing a badger is a wonderful privilege, but it is crucial to keep a safe distance when observing them so as not to alarm them or their sett. We first saw the badger through the patio door window, and it took no notice of me or Joanna as it walked past. I noticed it check beneath the bird feeders, probably for any food dropped or discarded by the birds, and it would do a full circuit of the garden before making its way to wherever it was headed. I remember one time when my dog, Saa, saw the badger as he lay by the door looking out on the garden. When he saw it climbing the three steps up onto the patio and walking towards him, I could see the confusion and curiosity in his face, as if to say, 'That's a funny-looking Border collie!' The badger completely ignored Saa as the dog looked on in disbelief.

I decided to set the trail camera to film the plinth feeding station so that I could capture footage of the birds. On one occasion, there was a woodpigeon happily going about its business, eating the seeds on the plinth, when a jackdaw came swooping into the garden straight towards it. When the jackdaw was within reach the pigeon jumped and took the stick that the jackdaw had in its beak – I'd never seen anything like it! I think the pigeon was as surprised as I was as the jackdaw paraded the stick around the plinth before flying away with it. I was looking out the patio door as it happened and I was so pleased that the trail camera caught it on film. Perfect timing for both trail camera and pigeon.

My garden is also filled with trees and plants, and most of them I either grew from cuttings or I split from other plants. My customers have kindly allowed me to take cuttings from their plants, as have friends and family. I'd never had the opportunity to do this sort of thing anywhere I'd lived before, so this opened up a whole different side to gardening for me, one I really enjoy! Buying plants from a garden centre can be very expensive, but creating a garden doesn't have to be. I've managed to grow salvias, roses, black elders, lavender, lemon verbenas and all sorts of plants from cuttings. It's surprisingly easy and very rewarding!

I also have a silver birch tree sitting on my patio in a large pot. I pulled it out of my customer's drive as a 2-inch weed and it is now over 4 feet tall. I love how the dappled light shimmers through its leaves: they are such beautiful trees. You don't need a big garden to enjoy a tree, and you certainly don't need to buy them as anyone can plant an acorn in a pot or repot a tree weed. I have so much more love for my plants and trees knowing I've grown them myself. I've planted my garden with the plants I like and plants that will, hopefully, attract all sorts of wildlife. As well as the plants I've just mentioned, I have buddleia (planted themselves), asters, helianthemums, rosemary, oxide daisies, crocosmia, daylilies, erigeron, rudbeckia, a spindle wood tree, cherry blossom and many more.

I also did some DIY in the garden to make a trough for a flowerbed. I had an old pallet, and bits from the old sheds I dismantled when we moved here along with other pieces of wood I'd saved 'just in case'. I used the pallet as the base, fixed two 4-foot 2″ x 2″ pieces of wood to the back and two to the front at the height I wanted the trough to be, building a frame. I then cut the shed panels to the lengths I needed to fix to the frame and fixed them with screws to create my own trough. Using bamboo canes I'd cut down from one of my jobs, I made cross-beams for a trellis, screwing them to the higher pieces of wood at the back of the trough. I placed a membrane material at the bottom of the trough to prevent the soil from falling through the gaps of the pallet, but allowing good drainage. I then filled it with compost.

It's not the most perfect-looking trough, as I cut and made everything by eye and by hand, but I like the rustic look. I placed it up against the house on the patio, right outside the door leading from my living room. The sofa is next to the patio door, so I get to look out onto the garden all the time. I enjoy watching the birds come and go and seeing our resident robins taking a bath in the waterfall of the pond or feeding from the feeders hanging from our cherry tree. We have blue tits, great tits, jackdaws, woodpigeons, sparrows and starlings, and of an evening, often before dark, Basil, my now-local fox, will make an appearance, checking the garden and having a drink from the pond before going on his way. I sometimes see the vixen fox or a squirrel, too. It's a treat to see such beautiful animals, and a wonderful show from the comfort of my sofa. I remember a quote I once heard: 'I could never be bored if I had a window to look out of.' I totally get that. It's about appreciating what you've got

A golden-hour portrait of Saa

Lavender and Roses – the flowers of summer – and Bob the robin

Chip the robin keeping lookout in the hazel tree

The dog fox with a bent tail and floppy ear, a regular visitor to Tony and Joanna's garden

A wood pigeon's head
and its peculiar eye

A portrait of
Basil the fox

*Above* Pip amongst the roses

*Left* A macro shot of Pip's eye

Pip posing in front of a foxglove and pink rose

Pip with the wind exposing his feathers underneath

Bobette perched among the blossom of the plum tree

*Right* Bobette posing with the autumn leaves as her backdrop

*Below* Bobette and Lucky pair up in anticipation of spring

*Left* The new visitor: a portrait of Lucky the robin

*Below* Forever friends: Bob the robin perched on Tony's hand

and what's around you. My mum once told me how she loved night-scented stock (*Matthiola longipetala*), or evening stock, as it's sometimes known. It has small purple flowers that emit an amazing scent in the evening, but there is no scent during the day. How nature works is amazing! With this in mind, I bought some stock as well as sweet pea seeds to grow up the trellis on the back of the trough. My hard work has certainly paid off, and the trough is now filled with colour. As I sit of an evening with the patio door open, the strong nostalgic scent of the stocks fills the air, and I can understand why my mum loves them so much. Smells can be a great reminder of times gone by and can bring back fond memories.

I also found a new passion for growing vegetables. We don't have the biggest veg patch, but we make the most of it by growing runner beans, sweetcorn, onions, tomatoes and anything else we can fit in there. I've found growing our own food to be very satisfying and it tastes so much better than supermarket food.

It doesn't matter what space you have. Any garden can be wildlife-friendly and contribute something to wider ecosystems – it doesn't need to cost a fortune. If you grow a tree in a pot and it gets too big, it can easily be rehomed to a big garden and then you can start again. Imagine how many more trees there would be if we all did that! You could also scatter wildflower seeds; they are easy to grow and excellent for insect life, which in turn supports the birds by increasing their sources of food.

Although Bob was gone I knew that the life of the garden continued, and that there were more birds to meet.

# Chapter Eight

# A New Visitor

One of the events that bonded Bob and me was when my dad was ill during the pandemic. The lockdown was a tough time for us all and I remember how hard it was not being able to go into the hospital with my dad. Bob stuck with me through all of that, but this time I didn't have Bob by my side.

I knew I had to share an old video of Bob on my socials for the wintry season so I shared some footage of him from a previous winter, perched on my hand eating a mealworm on a very cold, snowy day. I remember the day well. We'd had heavy snow the evening before, and the temperature was well below freezing! I waited for a few hours in the morning to ensure that the roads had been made safer by gritter lorries before making my way from Crowborough to Edenbridge to check on my little friend. I knew he wouldn't be able to find food for himself as everything was frozen solid and covered in snow.

It was a precarious drive, with cars abandoned everywhere – the drivers must've been caught out when the snow started unexpectedly the evening before. I'd never seen such devastation on the roads; there seemed to be a car up a bank or crashed into another around every bend! I took it slow to be sure that my car wasn't added to the list of casualties.

When I arrived in Edenbridge, to where Bob lived, I made my way to the plum tree, knowing that was where I was likely to find him. I could see him perched on his favourite branch, where I'd first met him, making clicking noises and fidgeting from side to side with excitement as I approached! I felt a massive sense of relief knowing that he was OK, but also a wave of emotion, seeing this tiny wild bird, who clearly knew who I was, being unable to contain his excitement when he saw me. It really hit home just how precious our bond and friendship was.

I held a mealworm between my finger and thumb, and Bob immediately flew to my hand and landed there. I could feel his icy cold claws tightly gripping my thumb as he helped himself to the mealworm. He must have felt my body heat as he stayed happily perched on my thumb for a minute or two.

Not only does this footage depict a Christmassy scene, with the snow and Bob the robin, it also shows kindness and friendship between two different species, love between beings – and hope. I decided that I would share footage of Bob to my socials every day throughout December. Even after all this time the love for him was still strong, and I'm sure it always will be.

In the present day, Bobette is following me around much more now, especially as the temperature is dropping and food is becoming harder to find. I often meet her on Bob's branch in the plum tree, and seeing her there gave me an idea. What if I could somehow balance Bob's book on a branch and encourage Bobette to stand next to it? I managed to wedge the book between a couple of branches, just where I had filmed and photographed Bob on so many previous occasions. Bobette then stood, quite happily, right in front of the red book with its drawing of Bob on the cover, and turned and looked straight at me as if she knew I wanted her to be there. So I took a few pictures and videos of her that I could share with my followers on social media. It felt a special moment for me, having Bob 'back in his plum tree', so to speak, and with his daughter, Bobette, standing next to him and now a part of his story and legacy. A family reunion for Christmas time felt right.

It was a different Christmas that year for my wife and I, as Joanna was planning to spend the season with her family in Poland, her first with them since before the Covid pandemic in 2020.

I decided to stay home to look after the dogs, especially as Pup had had a difficult few months with his back and back legs. Pup is 13 years old and has an underdeveloped hip, and arthritis is causing him more problems as he gets older – he can't go upstairs any more as he simply wouldn't make it. We have been working with our vet to treat him and make him as comfortable as possible and now, though it has taken a bit of working out, we have him enjoying life as best he can. So it was largely for this reason that I couldn't join Joanna. But I love spending Christmas with the dogs too and I don't know how many more Pup will have.

I took Joanna to the airport on Saturday 21 December, which happened to be the day of our 15th wedding anniversary! It was simply a coincidence, and we would celebrate on her return. The next day, Dave and Ashley, two of my best friends, came round for an English breakfast (cooked by me) and a good catch-up around the dining table. I don't have many close friends, but I enjoy every second I get to spend with those I have. We had drifted apart somewhat over the years, but that's how life goes – we all just got busy with our own lives. So we decided to try meeting up as much as possible throughout the year, even if it was just two or three times, and now, when we do, it's as if we only saw one another yesterday. In my opinion, these are the best type of friends you can have.

After breakfast we started up my old PlayStation 2, as we enjoy playing a game called *Mashed*. It's a racing game we can all play at the same time, and we've always found it entertaining, although I generally feel like the console picks on me and favours my friends. It has done for all the years we've played it – and that's going back to the early 2000s! We all like whiskey too, so we did have a bottle or two as the day went on. We also played my Nintendo 64, which I've had since the late 1990s, playing *Mario Kart* and even trying

*GoldenEye*. These were all games we played in the late 1990s, either together or with friends we no longer see as time has pushed us apart. As well as bonding over computer games, our friendship grew stronger through playing football for Chiddingstone. It wasn't just about playing for ourselves then, but about playing for our teammates. We battled hard together and lost, but we also battled hard and won, and we found that losing helped us appreciate the wins when they happened. Just as in the cold wintry days with the robins, we knew we were in it together, and sometimes that can build a bond and a sense of camaraderie that lasts a lifetime.

We also played board games that Dave brought round. I can't remember what they were, but we had fun playing them late into the night and into the early hours of the morning before calling it a night. Dave and Ash both stayed over and slept in the spare bedrooms. It really was a lovely day, playing games and catching up. It felt just like old times. They both left early the next morning, and I spent the day feeling excited about Christmas as I wrapped my nephew's presents for Christmas Day. I was looking forward to spending the holiday with all the family.

I was just settling down for the evening, about to watch *Wolf Hall*, when my mobile rang. I could see that it was my dad's number, which was a little unusual because he'd normally call me on the landline. I answered immediately as he'd had some health issues a month or two earlier, and I always made sure to respond quickly, especially after his aneurism scare in 2020.

It was as I feared. My stepmum, Alma, was on the line, and she said, 'Tony, your dad can't breathe, can you tell him he needs to go to hospital.' She then passed the phone to Dad, and he was literally gasping as he tried to speak. I told him that I would pick him up and take him to Pembury hospital. I knew this was going to be a long night as the hospitals are overstretched at the best of times, let alone over Christmas. I dropped Dad off at the A&E entrance as there was no way he would have been able to walk from the car park.

When I arrived in A&E it was full and I couldn't see him anywhere so I asked at the front desk and was directed to the right place. I could see Dad sitting at the end of the ward, which had been made into a makeshift waiting area with chairs for patients. It was where people with breathing difficulties were being sent for assessment and treatment.

When I got to my dad I could see that there were several people waiting to be seen by a doctor, some on oxygen and all with breathing difficulties. The other noticeable thing was that everyone had masks on except me and Dad – we hadn't been offered one and I didn't know where to get one. To see how much people were suffering and how much pressure the staff were under was certainly eye-opening.

There was a lady in the bed to our left who was clearly in a lot of pain with her chest. She asked every nurse who passed if she could have some painkillers, but for whatever reason I don't think she got any in all the time we were there. I heard the doctor telling her that she had a clot on her lung and just remember thinking how awful it all was: so many people struggling to breathe, people groaning in agony, their chests rattling. I did wonder how many of them would get to see Christmas, which was just three days away. Would my dad? A nurse approached and said to Dad, 'we're going to swab you to check if you have flu'. I went to find a toilet, and on my return I passed the nurse who had checked Dad. Handing me a mask, he remarked, 'you might want to put this on because your dad has the flu.' I obliged, of course.

From that moment, I knew my Christmas was over. There was no way I hadn't contracted flu; I felt fine at the time, but I knew it was coming. As we waited for Dad to be seen by a doctor, I sent my mum a text message explaining where I was and that I would probably miss Christmas with the family. My dad was eventually given a bed and placed on oxygen, with regular checks every 15 minutes or so. The doctor was not happy for him to go home because his oxygen levels were too low so he was admitted overnight. It was now after 1am and I was exhausted myself. I really needed to get back to the dogs as it wasn't fair leaving them for so long. I told my dad to call me if he needed anything, and I left him there for the night.

The next day, the doctors managed to get Dad's oxygen levels back to a safe level and he was discharged, so I picked him up and took him back to Alma. It was horrible seeing him suffering like that and I hoped I wouldn't be making any more hospital trips in the near future!

I woke up on Christmas morning and could feel my body starting to ache. Any slight movement was highly sensitive, and I knew my Christmas was going to be a quiet one. Before it got too bad, I mustered the energy to take the dogs for a nice long walk to the Ashdown Forest. But with every step I could feel my body deteriorating. This wasn't going to be a sniffily nose and a cold: this was proper flu, which I'd only had twice before in my life.

When we got home, I called Mum to confirm that I wouldn't be spending Christmas with her. I felt gutted and physically destroyed; it was clearly going to get worse before it got better. I told Ash and Dave via our WhatsApp group, and they both kept in touch, making sure I was OK as they knew I was on my own. They offered to drop round anything I needed, even though they live over 30 minutes away and were spending Christmas with their own families. I told them to stay away – I didn't want them to get flu – but it was very humbling to know I have such great friends who clearly cared about me.

Mum and Steve, my stepdad, drove over with

some food, so I spoke to them from a distance as they dropped it by my door and then backed off to the car. It was lovely to see them, albeit for just a minute. I thanked them gingerly and waved them farewell. As the hours passed, I found myself reflecting on Christmases gone by, fondly remembering my childhood when the magic was still so alive, and my brother and I couldn't sleep on Christmas Eve because the excitement was just too much! I also thought of loved ones who have gone, friends and family no longer at the dinner table enjoying the festive feast, those empty spaces now greeted with sadness as younger family members know only a name but not a face.

I thought of how we can share memories of those we miss with the next generation and create a legacy for them. I hope that is what I have managed to do with Bob's book, sharing our story and its messages with others so that they, too, can experience his unique personality and the hope he represented for me, even though they won't get to meet him themselves.

The last time my dad was ill was when he unexpectedly had a stroke in early summer 2020. A very strange thing had happened the day before. Bob had disappeared from the garden for the first time a couple of weeks before, in early May, and had not returned. I had just started to become resigned to the idea that he might have left for new territory with better food sources and places for shelter, when, on 4 June, he reappeared. It was the next day that I received the news that Dad had suffered a brain aneurysm, and the weeks and months following were a very difficult time in my life: I was so worried about Dad but unable to visit him due to lockdown restrictions. Seeing Bob everyday was a light during the darkness.

This time, though, I'd been able to be with my dad for a bit, help with lifts to the hospital, and make sure that he was OK. I felt grateful for the change in the world's circumstances that allowed this to happen, even though this time I didn't have Bob to help me through it. It was another reminder, along with the ever-growing and ever-changing garden, that the world keeps turning despite our own sorrows and worries.

I also kept thinking about Dad and the other people I'd seen at A&E. I was pleased Dad was home with Alma and not in hospital over Christmas, but I did wonder if the lady with the clot on her lung had survived and what had happened to the others. I knew I would get over the flu, so how could I really moan when the hospital was full of people unable to go home? Plus, Pup and Saa were with me, so I wasn't really alone.

* * *

I returned to work on 7 January, and it was as if I'd never been away. This also marked over two years of me knowing Bobette as I'd met her in December 2022, and Bob disappeared the following April. I still believed that Bobette was Bob's daughter because of their similarities. Bob had a small white patch in the orange on his chest, on the left-hand side, or on the right-hand side if looking at him face on. This patch was only ever visible at certain times, however: sometimes his chest was completely orange with no sign of it. It would all depend on how his feathers were sitting at any given time. A robin's feathers move all the time – puffed up when they are cold, streamlined and hugged tight to their body if they are feeling threatened. As I got to know Bobette, I noticed that she had the same white patch in exactly the same place as Bob, and that, just as with Bob, the patch was only visible at certain times! Of course, I could never prove that Bobette is Bob's daughter. It could simply be a coincidence. But it is a lovely thought.

It was a cold, frosty morning, and Bobette

greeted me on the picket fence just as Bob had so often done before her. I offered her a mealworm, and she gladly took it from me and flew off into the garden with her breakfast.

In the spring of 2024, Bobette had paired up with a new male robin who occupied the patio area from the top of the lawn to the main house, adjoining Bobette's territory. I assume the male robin who is there now is the same one, although I can't be certain as he makes very little effort to interact with me. Where I park my van puts me more in his territory, but this hasn't stopped Bobette from greeting me in the mornings by landing on my wing mirror and enjoying a mealworm or two as I have my coffee before starting work.

The male robin seemed to mildly disapprove of having Bobette in his territory, as he would alert us to his presence by making whiney, squeaky noises from the safety of the picket fence. Bobette would take no notice whatsoever, though, and nothing ever came of it. He never challenged her and there was never any fighting. There certainly could have been fighting, even if they were former partners, but it makes little sense to risk unnecessary injury. If food had been scarce and times been harder, things may have been different. In any case, just as Bob did, she would come flying over to greet me when she heard my van pull up.

Throughout January, I worked in the garden next door, which is where I usually park my van. This property is also part of the estate, so I maintain and look after their garden too sometimes. It needed a good tidy as it had been neglected a bit for a year or so by the previous tenants. Weeds were growing from the brick block paving that went round the house, the flowerbeds were wildly overgrown with weeds, nettles and thistles, and bellbine had completely taken over – so I had my work cut out!

Bobette would often join me there as I worked, settling on the wheelbarrow, garden fork or a nearby shrub. She'd even sit on the toe of my boot if I sat down to take a few minutes' break. It was a lovely feeling knowing she was comfortable enough around me to do that, just as Bob and Bobbin used to do.

I was still working in the main garden, too, although most of my time was spent next door during the early months of the year. When I was in the main garden, and if I was anywhere near the old plum tree, Bobette would still greet me there, just as Bob used to do. The plum tree isn't too far from next door's garden, so she is still in her own territory or at least not too far from it.

We hadn't gone unnoticed. I was working mostly around the back, with Bobette and Pup and Saa for company, but when I started on the part of the garden that is at the front of the house, I was working near to where I park my van. It was then that another robin made itself known! This one was happy to land on my fork, the wheelbarrow or anything nearby to be able to see what I was doing. As I faced the house, I'd sometimes have Bobette to the right of me and the other robin to the left. This area seemed to be something of a no man's land for the birds: neither seemed to control it as their territory. I knew the new robin wasn't the individual with whom Bobette had, I thought, paired up the previous year, simply because *that* robin would watch the other two from the safety of his territory on the picket fence!

One thing I noticed about the new robin was that he was very vocal: he seemed to love singing and would do so all day long! It was like having my very own 'robin jukebox'. I never listen to the radio or any music when I'm at work, come to think of it. Why would I want to? I have the beautiful songs of the birds to fill my ears with the best music there is – the sound of nature!

The new robin would sometimes clash with Bobette, and there would be a little chasing or singing to let the other know of their displeasure. But it was never too aggressive or serious.

Both male and female robins sing, both with equal complexity, and mainly to defend their territories from potential rivals. The male robin also watched as Bobette would confidently take mealworms from my hand. I offered him one at times too, and it was clear that he wanted to take it, but he just couldn't find the courage to do it. So I'd drop a few on the ground in his direction and he would happily help himself.

Sometimes I would get confused about who was who, but I'd quickly see the difference. Firstly, Bobette has the white patch on her chest, although not always visible; and secondly, she is so much calmer and more relaxed than the other robin. She also doesn't sing as much. It only took a matter of days before 'Pip' (named by our followers on social media) built up the confidence to take food from my hand, and he very quickly became a fond part of the robin family.

# Chapter Nine

# The Power of Trust

February brought with it a shift in territories. Bobette paired up with the robin who owned the territory next to the picket fence, the same one, I believe, that she paired up with last year. He has now moved into her territory and has abandoned his own. Pip has now moved into and claimed the other robin's territory. Last year Bobette left her territory by the plum tree to join the same robin, but in his territory; curiously, this year it is the other way around.

On Valentine's Day I popped in to see the robins. My wife was at work, and I had some spare time, so what better way to spend it! There is a small seating area on the left of the main patio as you look from the house. A few years ago my customer and I made a table using a granite worktop from their old kitchen, which we thought too good to throw away. We placed the worktop onto two small barrels and that was it. The granite is so heavy we didn't need to affix it – it wasn't going anywhere! With two benches added for seating, it has become the perfect coffee-table-sized outdoor table and seating area.

During the summer, one of the barrels was also home to wild honeybees, which was great to watch – the bees went in and out from the hole where the cork would once have been. The bees never attacked or caused us any problems, even when we sat at the table. They would fly in and out of the hive, busy collecting pollen and nectar, and were fascinating to observe.

This area of the garden was now Pip's territory, and I knew that he wouldn't be able to resist seeing what I was up to. I had in mind trying to film him with Bob's book – it's always nice to get footage, if I can, of one of the robins landing on it. I usually open the book and stand it upright so that the robin is standing on the top above the title, with Bob's image below. Pip is nearly always twittering or singing, so I really hoped he'd do so here! As predicted, Pip came to check out what I was doing. As I placed the book on the table, he was flitting from the table to the bench and back again, but I did not expect what happened next. It wasn't Pip who landed on the book but Bobette, who'd decided to join us! They certainly knew each other, but they were not a breeding pair. I really didn't know how this would play out. Robins can be extremely territorial and I really hoped that they wouldn't fight, especially as Bobette had so blatantly invaded Pip's space!

I was able to film the moment, with Bobette perched on the book and Pip, at first, standing in close proximity, before flying to the bench next to me. Although Bobette had invaded Pip's territory, he did not challenge her – nor she him – but she certainly had the more dominant air, with a calm matriarchal aura about her. Perhaps Pip is one of her offspring from a previous year, or maybe she's just the older, wiser, more dominant bird whose presence simply demands respect.

I don't know. But I do know that it was a lovely thing to witness and experience, especially on Valentine's Day.

* * *

My love of photography returned as my grief for Bob took on a new flavour. There was never a point when I forgot about Bob, but the new life in the garden reminded me that there are always more moments to enjoy. So I would often be on the lookout for photo opportunities. In the garden near the house there is a large terracotta urn in one of the flowerbeds. It's an ornamental piece to give structure to the bed and has been there for over 15 years, all the time I have worked here. Pip favours standing on the rim of the urn to sing his songs – his voice then projects across the lawn and down the garden! – and this meant that he'd be at waist height to me, great for taking his picture. I like my photos to be as sharp as possible, but my hands are not as steady as they were and it's becoming more difficult to avoid camera shake, which can lead to soft photos. With Pip at waist height, I could kneel on one leg and rest my elbow on the other when holding the camera steady.

The eyes are always my focal point. When photographing any animal or person, the eyes are what draw you into the picture, so in my view that's what should be in focus. I rested the camera on the edge of the urn to take Pip's photo as he stood there. For the first couple, I was roughly a foot away, capturing the top half of his body. It was slightly windy, so in the photos you can see his chest feathers being blown up, and it looked as if he was wearing a ruff. The intricate details of the feathers are amazing: you can see all the little patterns, with his orange ruff being blown under his chin. It's fascinating to note that the breast feathers are only orange on the tips – the rest of the feather is a very dark grey! I guess I'd never given this much thought. If a feather fell out it wouldn't be as striking as one might imagine – dark grey with an orange tip, quite unassuming – but layer them together and you've got this beautiful, bright-orange-breasted little bird!

These photographs were great, but with Pip so relaxed, I decided to get even closer and see if he'd stay still long enough for me to take a photo of his eye with my macro lens. I moved the camera closer, keeping it on the rim of the urn for support. This was crucial, because the closer I got the more any movement would be magnified because of the lens. Focusing on his eye, keeping as steady as possible, I waited for him to be completely still. I took a number of photos, adjusting my position slightly each time in the hope of capturing a clear image of his eye. I was not disappointed. The details were truly stunning: the tiniest orange feathers intricately surround his black eyelids, and his dark brown eye and black pupil reflect the sky and landscape, with the blue sky and a silver birch tree clearly visible in the reflection. The robin really is a true wonder of the natural world.

* * *

Once again, the garden is in full bloom as spring is well underway. It's been a dry, warm start to the season and the blossoms are plentiful, reflecting the settled conditions. Bob's plum tree, now part of Bobette's territory, is looking a picture, with its white blossoms covering every branch, and the deafening hum of bees collecting nectar and pollen as the anticipation of new life fills the air! The daffodils – thousands of them (many of which I planted over the years), fill the grass islands surrounding the fruit trees in the orchard, and the fresh, rich green of the grass, the fruit trees in bloom and the daffs bring nothing but excitement and optimism for the year to come! I love seeing the haze appear on the trees as they start bursting into leaf, and how the dull wintry coat is gradually shaken off by the vibrantly saturated colour of life filtering back into the landscape.

I face the main garden, knowing I'm likely to

bump into Bobette as she has a keen eye and generally knows when I'm around. She has nested in the outbuilding again – I've watched her going in and out – as she did last year. She accesses the building from the area where I park my car, through some holes in the roof, and has no trouble getting in or out.

The outbuilding is used for storage, among other things, and I often go in there myself. On this occasion, when I went in Bobette was there too, on one of the beams in the roof. I stood completely still as I watched her. I knew the nest must be up there somewhere, and although she knows me I never want to be responsible for any mishaps with her young. The building is too important for us to stop using, and she knows we go in and out all the time, but if I see her in there, I take extra care not to startle her, and I certainly don't take any interest in the nest. Bobette knew I was there, and I could hear her babies calling her from high up in the beams. I watched as she disappeared out of sight, and then came the shrill of a satisfied baby: Bobette must have given it some food! It put a smile on my face to know that she has one or more youngsters waiting to fledge and to continue her family line!

It's not the first time I've walked in on a feathered family. One spring morning, I opened the door to the woodstore, which is situated next to the vegetable garden. The logs for firewood are stacked along the back, and to the right we keep all sorts of wood, from fence posts and planks to anything that might come in handy. There was also a pile of cut planks, neatly stacked around waist height immediately to the right. As I walked in, I was greeted by five grumpy-looking small birds, huddled together on top of the planks. It was a bit of an 'oh, hi' moment – I felt as if I'd walked in on someone at an inappropriate time! I couldn't help but smile as the family of wrens stared back at me.

Wrens have markedly different breeding

patterns to robins. While the two species mate and breed at the same times of year, it is the male wrens who build the nests. They work very hard early in the spring and will build multiple nests for the purpose of attracting females. The females then inspect the nests in order to choose the right mate. The males are also polygamous throughout the breeding season: if multiple females choose their nests, then they could have multiple broods with each of them.

These baby wrens weren't in their nest or with an adult male or female, but must've fledged not long before I saw them. They clearly hadn't yet built up the courage to leave the safety of the shed. I slowly backed back out, trying not to make any sudden movements, and then gently closed the door, forgetting about whatever it was I went in there for. I think it goes to show that trust between a gardener and the animals in the garden has to be maintained, and that considerate behaviour on the part of the gardener is crucial.

There was one time when I worried that I'd broken the trust of Bobette. Once, as I approached her, I accidentally tripped and stumbled. My movement would, I think, have been deemed by her to be out of character, and perhaps mildly aggressive. She flinched back a little and immediately raised her left leg, almost in a submissive way, as if to remind me that we trust each other and are friends! She kept her foot tucked into her belly. After recovering my footing, I offered her a mealworm, as I normally would, and she gratefully took it and flew off. She promptly returned and took up the same pose of standing on one leg again, which I believe was a sign of trust. Thankfully, rather than harming our relationship I think the episode only strengthened it.

The way I trust and care for Bobette reminded me of my friendships when I was younger. I remember my mum and her friend, Frances, deciding that my brother and I and Frances's three children were to attend a children's play scheme at a primary school that we were not familiar with. I remember not wanting to go – I didn't need such things. I was more than happy entertaining myself, playing outside on our estate. We had fields, ponds, our bikes and, most importantly, the company of our friends. None of us wanted to be there.

No sooner had we said goodbye to our mums than we decided to run along the side of the school building and make our way to the playground. As we reached open space, a girl came running along the other side of the building and we collided. I came off much worse as she ran into the side of me, her knee connecting with the side of my left knee. I remember hitting the ground and thinking 'OUCH!!' I don't know if you've ever done the same and experienced that moment when you can't move, and you're unsure of the damage done. Well, that is what it was like. I was used to scraping my knees, falling off my bike and so on. I was an outdoor kid: I knew my limits and I knew when something was wrong.

I was helped up by my brother and his friend Ross, who had seen what had happened. I knew Ross well; he was in my brother's year, a year older than me, and he lived next door to my nan and grandad. Edenbridge is a small town, with a population of around eight thousand, so everyone knew everyone. I couldn't put weight on my leg nor could I walk, so Ross carried me, literally like a baby, to the people running the play scheme. He and my brother stayed with me while the first aider examined me and declared me to be OK. I remember saying, 'I'm not OK, I think you should call my dad.' They declined and told us to go back outside and play.

I still couldn't walk, so Ross carried me wherever we went. He did this for three hours. The breaking point came when he put me down on a bench outside the school building because he wanted to go somewhere, but he made sure that

I was alright first. From the bench I could see my brother inside the school hall, and I decided that I was going to get him to make the teachers call our dad. I'd had enough now: my leg was really swollen and I couldn't walk. I hopped to the wall of the building with my injured leg stretched out in front of me – I couldn't bend it – and, as I got to the hall entrance, I had the sudden realization that there was no more wall to hold onto. So I decided to try to walk. I cannot describe the pain I felt as I put weight on my injured knee. It was like a twig snapping beneath me. I fell to the ground and cried, not only from the pain but also the feeling of helplessness. I can't remember how I ended up back in the first-aid room, but I do remember what happened next! For some reason I was sitting on top of a unit which went around the edges of the little room, with my leg stretched out on the unit, and my back against the wall. This was a relief because my knee was so swollen I couldn't bend my leg at all. This time the head teacher was there as well as other adults, and again they decided I would be fine, and that I just needed to walk it off. They said, 'We'll all be going to the leisure centre soon, we're sure you'll be able to swim it off.' I remember this overwhelming feeling of deflation and defeat. I'd always considered myself a bit of a battler, but this had finished me.

My main thought was, 'There is no way I am going to be able to walk to the leisure centre even if it is a few hundred yards up the road, and there is certainly no way I could swim if I make it there!' There was only one option left. I turned on the waterworks and begged them to call my dad. They finally agreed, and Dad was there within ten minutes. He took one look at my knee, said, 'That's obviously broken', and took me straight to Kent and Sussex hospital in Tunbridge Wells. I had to stay the night because the knee was still swelling and they didn't want to put a cast on it as the pressure could build inside. I spent six weeks, the whole of the summer holidays, in a plaster cast, from the top of my thigh to my toes. I'd been *sure* that I hadn't wanted to go to that play scheme, and I never went to one again.

This incident probably helped mould my personality a bit. I am very independent and like to stay in control of everything I do, and I pay great attention to detail. My trust has to be earned.

I think my independence helps me to relate to the robins and the other wildlife in the garden more meaningfully. They, too, are cautious around people and do not trust you immediately – you have to prove to them that you deserve it. I respect their space, and their need for some distance, and only ever get closer to them when they have approached me.

* * *

The robins are all very busy hunting for food to feed their young as their first broods are readying themselves to fly the nest. The consistently warm weather has provided an abundance of insects, which has made parenting a little easier than it sometimes is if there's a cold snap or a rainy spell in March or April. So the robins have had a good head start this breeding season. Sometimes the robins like to show off and show me their catch! One afternoon, on my way home from another job, I popped in to see the robins as I so often do. I made my way to the veg garden to see if Bobette was about, and as I went through the gate she landed on the fence. I could see that she had something in her beak, and I was able to identify it as a wolf spider. She proudly paraded it in front of me, long enough for me to film her, and then she was off! I saw her go into the outbuilding, so I can only assume that the spider made a good meal for one of her young. This reminded me of when Bob used to join me in the veg garden: the spiders always seemed to be his favourite choice of meal too.

Pip was also proving to be a great dad and

provider, often showing me his beak full of bugs! One morning, as I was enjoying my coffee before starting work, Pip landed on the wing mirror of my van with his beak full of critters. I couldn't identify them all, but the bright green caterpillar was obvious as it wriggled in vain to escape: it looked like Pip was sporting a bright green moustache! It was great to know that the robins were doing an amazing job as parents. I don't know why they felt the need to show me their catch. Maybe it was just habit to interact with me regardless of what they were doing; maybe they hoped I'd give them more food, even if their beaks were already full; or maybe they simply wanted to show me how skilled they were as hunters. But it was lovely to be included and to be able to see first-hand what they were catching for their young! I felt so proud of them and the tireless work they do to provide for their offspring, especially after seeing how they endure the harshness of winter. I can only admire their resilience and work ethic.

* * *

May also brought my first glimpse of Bobette's babies. Her first brood had now flown the nest, and I managed to film one as it kept a low profile in the yew hedge. It kept perfectly still, with a grumpy look on its face (baby birds naturally do look very grumpy – it's comical), and I could see its speckled brown breast. I didn't interact with the baby robin – I was being careful not to disrupt it at such an early stage in its development – but it was such a pleasure to see it.

Bobette now started on the second brood as her partner provided most of the food for the fledglings. Bobette's partner had never shown any interest in me; he always stayed back. I couldn't positively identify the male robin as being the same one as last year, but as his behaviour was the same I'd assumed that it was. Bobette would still seek me out if she wanted an easy meal. She was working tirelessly to raise her family, but to my surprise, now the fledglings had become the responsibility of her partner. One day he followed Bobette, watched her take food from me, and then showed an interest in wanting an easy meal himself, so I offered him a mealworm and he didn't hesitate. He flew straight to my hand and took it from me! This was so heartwarming! It goes to show that he trusted his partner's judgement. He must've really needed that little boost as he only did this a couple of times, and then withdrew as per usual and kept his distance. We often assume that animals don't have complex emotions but I think they are more clever than we give them credit for. Trust is not just something relevant to humans.

The trust between Pip and me at this time was also growing stronger. In early June, the flowerbeds were bursting with colour, and Pip followed me around everywhere. I was spending much of my time working in his territory, keeping the flowerbeds looking immaculate, deadheading the roses and keeping the weeds at bay. I saw in this an opportunity for a photoshoot with Pip, just as I had with Bobbin a couple of years ago with the poppies. I knew Pip would willingly oblige so I got to work! I used the same wooden-handled half moon as the prop for him to perch on as I'd used for Bobbin. The flowers looked wonderfully fresh and vibrant as I took pictures among the Californian poppies, foxgloves, peonies, lavender and roses. Pip was very easy and enjoyable to work with, and the results were lovely with the colourful, vivid backdrops. Because robins are closely linked to winter some people believe that they are only around during the winter months in the UK. We see endless photos of puffed-up robins on a cold, frosty day, the vibrant red breast standing out in the snow, but the truth is that most robins are with us all year round here – only a minority migrate. It was lovely to do a summer shoot with Pip, and to show something a little different from the norm. And I think Pip enjoyed the attention too.

* * *

When I started secondary school at the end of the summer holidays after breaking my leg, my world looked very different from before. My parents were getting divorced, and I was out of the plaster cast but still needed crutches to walk because of the muscle wastage from being in the cast for so long. I was cautious with my left knee for years after, and I wouldn't kick a football with my 'bad' leg. When I could walk properly, I started playing football with my friends at school, and after school with my brother and our friends on our estate. Mick Burns, who lived three doors down from us, saw us playing one day and asked if we'd like to learn how to play football properly.

Mick, who was in his sixties, arranged to train us youngsters every Thursday after school and we loved it! Word spread quickly and soon our friends from all over town were coming every Thursday to play football, boys and girls, all to be trained by Mick. I remember getting there once, eagerly anticipating a match, and Mick turned to us all and said, 'You won't be playing football today, you will be playing netball.' We all moaned and groaned, perplexed as to why. However, it turned out to be one of the greatest lessons we ever learned about football, because it taught us how to play as a team rather than as individuals. In netball, the person with the ball cannot move, so it is down to their teammates to move into space to give the person with the ball options. Mick knew what he was doing, and we all respected him greatly, and the Thursday afternoon football club went on for years.

Years later, I saw Mick sitting on his front doorstep one hot summer's day as I pulled up in my van. Like many of the people I remember from childhood, he still lived in the same house. I cut the grass for the lady opposite, so I saw him often. Mick, now into his eighties, had trouble walking, and he had recently lost his wife, whom he adored. It was so sad seeing him there, so I went over, remembering everything he'd done for us as kids, and said hello. He was a guy I'd always known to be happy and full of life but he was a broken man. After he acknowledged me fondly, he said something that still haunts me. He asked, in a very sad tone, 'What's the point of it all, Tone?' This man who was struck by grief and the weight of the world couldn't make sense of anything. It was heartbreaking. I didn't know what to say, so I simply replied, 'I've no idea, Mick.'

Mick passed away in 2024. I was so sad to hear the news, as were so many of us Thursday football lads and lasses. But deep down I knew that he'd had enough, so in other ways I felt relief for him. I attended his funeral and, in his eulogy, his daughter made reference to a group of youngsters who would knock on the door every Thursday to see if he was coming out to play. The hairs on the back of my neck stood up and I felt a lump in my throat: that was us she was talking about. Even after all these years it must've been a fond memory for him, just as it was for all us kids. The kindness of one man went a long way.

When Mick could no longer cut his own lawn, I would do it for him when I did his neighbour's. I always refused payment: it was the least I could do after all he had done for us as kids. Small acts of kindness may always be offered in return for what others have done for us.

# Chapter Ten

# The Dawn Chorus

Watching the sunrise is a great way to start the day, and I usually try to get to work just before the sky burns with the anticipation of a new day. Pip has taken to standing on a fence post to participate in the dawn chorus, and of course I get a front-row seat as he entertains all those willing to listen! The sun slowly rising behind him as he sings, I have a clear view across the field to the horizon, as a fine mist lightly obscures the view of a large solitary oak tree standing there. I can only guess how many sunrises that tree has witnessed as it welcomes another one.

The sky changes from a vibrant magenta to a fiery orange as the sun slowly creeps over the horizon, the stillness in the air giving way to movement as the birdsong intensifies. It's difficult to identify the individual species as they all seem to be trying to outdo one another, but the sequence appears to be as follows. It starts with the high-pitched singing of the robins, blackbirds and thrushes, which is then undercut by the lower coos of the woodpigeon, which somehow fits in perfectly, along with the wrens and warblers. Finally, as it gets light enough for them to see, the great tits, blue tits and sparrows join in with the best concert I'm ever likely to witness. And it's all for free – not just for me but for everybody!

Pip acts as if we've been friends for years. He's a very confident robin, and he has fitted himself into my routine with ease – another little personality, so different from all the others. One morning, some time after sunrise, I was weeding the flowerbeds in the main garden, which I'd neglected for most of the winter as I'd tried to get next door's garden into better shape. I decided to take five minutes to have a little rest so I flipped my weeding bucket upside down on the lawn and sat on it with my feet crossed and my legs stretched out in front of me. I was facing out onto the lawn where Pup and Saa were already lying down side by side.

Pip, being the confident robin he was, decided to join me, and not only that: he perched on one of my boots and proceeded to twitter away. It was as if he was having a conversation with me, telling me everything he wanted me to know in a continuous gentle melody. It was lovely listening to him, and to watch him with his beak slightly open – I could see his throat moving with every note. You can picture the scene. I had Pip perched on my boot, Pup and Saa were lying on the lawn in front of me, roughly 20 feet away and looking in my direction, and Pip was positioned between them as he sang. I decided to film the moment of course, as I had my phone in my pocket, and I shared the feel-good clip with my followers on social media.

* * *

In the summer, my wife and I were invited by the SongBird Survival charity to the famous Chelsea Flower Show in London, and we went in support for their cause. The charity had their own garden there to help raise awareness about songbirds in the UK and to highlight their rapid decline. The garden was stocked with native plants: some to provide shelter, some for food, and even some plants that can retain water in its foliage, which could be a lifeline for certain birds during the summer. The charity does research into the decline of the songbird population and advocates for ways we can all help. The robin is a songbird, and although they are not struggling in numbers like some of their counterparts are, they are well loved and easily recognizable because of their bright orange breast and friendly nature, so they are a great representative when it comes to spreading the word about the songbird's plight.

The term songbird actually has a very specific scientific meaning, although we may use it quite loosely. These birds belong to a group known as passerines. They have a highly developed voice box that allows them to sing complex songs and are the birds that join in the dawn chorus. They are also perching birds, with feet that are adapted to sit on branches and other thin surfaces (like the rim of an urn, for example).

We had a lovely evening with the charity and I think there are many ways we can all help the cause. For example, nest boxes are an easy and affordable thing to add to your garden. Now that there are fewer places available to birds to nest in, these can really support birds at the start of nesting season and encourage them into our gardens. The right nest box will depend on the kind of birds you want to attract: boxes with a smaller hole will be best for blue tits, coal tits or marsh tits, while larger holes will work for larger birds such as great tits, tree sparrows and flycatchers. We should also think about the positioning of the box: fledglings can fall when first leaving the nest, so planting a hedge below the box can give cushioning or shelter from predators. SongBird Survival also recommend leaving food out for birds in the winter months only, and in the summer to focus on providing fresh, clean water for them daily.

Next time you hear the dawn chorus, remember the songbirds we have to thank for it, and remember the power we have to help them in our own spaces.

* * *

I hadn't seen much of Pip since 24 June, when he'd kept me company for most of the day as I weeded and swept the drive. It's a large, bricked drive with sand swept between each brick, so the weeds grow like mad and it can take a few hours to get it looking nice. Pip watched what I was doing from the stone troughs situated around the edges of the drive. The troughs are planted with annuals – nicotiana, geraniums and osteospermum, among others – to add a bit of colour and interest to the parking area. He also perched on the watering can handle by the tap, or landed on the bucket where

I'd put the pulled-up weeds. As always, he was great company.

On this particular morning, I arrived at 5.30am and had a coffee in the van as I always do. Often I am joined by Pip, especially during late spring and into summer, but today, as for the past few weeks, there was no sign of him. I finished my coffee by 5.45am, let the dogs out the van, and filled their water bowl and a watering can using the outside tap from the main house. Then I made my way to the plum tree with the watering can. I always put fresh water in the tray, which is situated under the hedge, and in the birdbath by the plum tree. Bobette made herself known and was happy to interact with me. This wasn't happpening as often as it used to since her fledglings had left and breeding season seemed to be over. But she would appear at least once a day when I was at work and, even if she didn't want a mealworm, would still get my attention, as if to say 'Hi, I'm still here, don't forget about me!' She looked as if she was starting her annual moult, so she would be cautious, and understandably so, because she is far more vulnerable without a full body of feathers! She took a mealworm from me and let me film her for a few seconds.

I spent part of the morning weeding and cutting back perennials that had finished flowering. I do this to encourage new growth and possibly a second flowering or bloom as perennials are so often obliging like that.

My customer called me just after 11am for our morning coffee on the patio together. It had been raining, although nothing too serious – just the odd sharp shower. I sat in my usual place at the garden table with my back to the flowerbed, and my customer sat next to me. We were there for no more than a minute when I felt the air move as bird wings flapped close to my head! My customer said, 'Was that Pip? I haven't seen him for a while.' As he spoke I heard the unmistakable sound of a robin clicking in the flowerbed behind me. I turned to look, but I couldn't see anything, and then, out of nowhere, Pip flew from the flowerbed and landed right next to my head and settled on the back of my chair! With a big grin on my face, I said, 'Hello Pip, nice to see you,' then put some mealworms on the table for him, something my customer has also been doing for Pip throughout the year.

Pip did look a little worse for wear. He looked as if he'd been caught in the rain or had had a bath somewhere and his tail was missing! This would explain why I hadn't seen much of him: he was going through his annual moult, so he'd been keeping a low profile to avoid predators. This must have meant that Pip's offspring had also fledged and moved on, although I never did see his babies, who'd done a good job of keeping out of sight. I think the nest was over the fence somewhere, out the front of the house, as I saw Pip going in that direction on many occasions with his beak full of bugs, presumably to feed his young. I also saw his partner doing the same, and saw her with Pip on many occasions, but she never interacted with me. My customer was clearly pleased to see Pip too!

Unlike Bob, who was very much a one-person robin and would do his best to avoid others, Pip is the complete opposite. He has won the hearts of everyone. My customer gleefully told me about the time he had a shock as he was sitting on the sofa in the conservatory, with the doors open, reading his paper. Something caught his eye and when he looked down, there was Pip happily perched on his foot! Since that day it's safe to say that Pip has become part of the family, and not just my robin family, but the household's too.

* * *

The following week, I'd just finished weeding the paths, and decided to have a cup of coffee. I sat on a bench in the brick paved area very near the plum tree in Bobette's territory. As I was looking at my phone, I felt something land on my left leg near my knee. Surprised, I looked up to see Bobette perched on my leg looking at me. I just had to smile. She had landed on my leg once before when she'd joined me in the van, but it had never happened outside! I remained calm and avoided any unnecessary movement for fear of spooking her, and as I already had my phone in my hand, I took the opportunity to do a live video on Instagram. It was really nice to be able to share such a moment with our followers as it was happening in real time.

The bench became the place where we met, just as the plum tree had been the place where I'd so often meet Bob. It was lovely that Bobette was still happy to interact with me, and, as the years go by, I feel that our bond is getting stronger. Bobette is certainly the robin sweetheart of my social media pages, though everyone loves Pip too with his happy-go-lucky ways and constant singing – it's difficult not to love them both.

Bobette seems to quite enjoy being filmed, and she certainly knows how to pose in front of the camera, just as Bob did. Once when I was filming her, the top half of her body suddenly clicked up and down – it sounded like the firing of a camera shutter. I could only assume that it was a hiccup, or that she'd become a walking camera! It was an amusing thing to witness, and I am so pleased that I managed to capture the moment on film. It turns out, however, that as birds have no diaphragm it is impossible for them to hiccup! Birds have been documented doing similar things though, and it is thought that it could be due to respiratory irritation – so perhaps closer to a cough than a hiccup! She was standing on the seat of the bench, which made her look tiny and really put into perspective just how small robins actually are. It was a light moment of relief ahead of what was to come.

* * *

August was a very hot and dry month; it didn't rain at all. I took a two-week holiday midway through to rest and to get some work done in my own garden. Of course, just as I did with Bob, when the weather was extreme, I became concerned about the robins. I popped in to see them a few times during my holiday, primarily to ensure that their water sources were full and to offer them some food if they wanted it. Pip and Chip seemed perfectly fine throughout, but on one occasion when I found Bobette she looked as if she was really struggling. I found her on the floor by the bench where we normally meet; with her colouration she blended in perfectly with the fallen fruit and leaves from the crab-apple tree.

The trees, stressed by the persistent heat and dry weather, were dropping their leaves early, creating a false autumn. Bobette knew I was there as she stood among the fallen leaves and fruit. I knelt next to her, offering her a mealworm, and she took it from me and then remained standing, motionless as she struggled to keep her eyes open. Eventually her eyes shut completely. Just as I'd done with Bob on that cold February morning back in 2023, I felt as if I was her protector during a moment of vulnerability. There was a feeling of complete trust that I would do her no harm. I cannot put into words what that moment felt like. There was a sense of pride mixed with worry, and time stood still – it was just the two of us, albeit briefly. After a minute or two she woke up and hopped into the yew hedge next to where she was standing. I refreshed her water supplies, topped up the birdbath, and replenished the seed tray I leave under the mixed hedge near the plum tree.

Bobette heard me pouring the water. She revived herself enough to hop out from under the hedge and flew up to the birdbath where she enjoyed a nice, fresh drink. She was so graceful in the way she drank, putting her beak into the water and then tilting her head back as she seemed to taste every drop with the satisfying movement.

It may seem like a small thing but providing water for our songbirds in the summer months really does make a difference. Remember to use a shallow dish to avoid the possibility of them drowning or put some rocks in the water so that the birds can use them to climb out if they need to. We want these birds to be around for many more years to come so remember to care for them when you hear that dawn chorus.

When September arrives, Bobette has no young to worry about, and food is plentiful, with insects and bugs everywhere! I consider this part of the year as one when the robins can relax a little: it is probably the easiest period for them, before the struggle of winter begins. They have finished moulting, so are fully feathered with a healthy, fresh new set, making them fast and agile again, and also well protected for the winter to come, and they have no young to feed, or any partner to worry about. The temperatures are far more bearable than the overwhelming heat of high summer, and there is plenty of food, with fallen fruit attracting flies that feast on the rotting flesh. Life seems good for the robins for this short window of time. The most important thing for them now is to keep hold of their territory.

# Chapter Eleven

# A Surprising Visitor

The anticipation of autumn hangs in the air. The days are getting shorter, the leaves are starting to turn, the mornings are cooler, and the sun is lower in the sky, creating a lovely light to film the robins, with fewer harsh shadows.

Bobette has been more vocal than normal, letting off random chirps, a little like the calls she'd make in spring but at a deeper pitch. She has also been very chatty with continuous melodies and twittering, probably to ensure that any robins nearby know that this is her territory and that this is where she will be for the winter to come.

My days have become much busier again as the grass is growing tall and lush. I like to keep the lawns cut, especially as they grow so fast at this time of the year, and when the leaves start to fall, they make the job all the harder as they fill the mower box in no time. I spend most of the day walking back and forth to the compost bins to empty the box. It is the time of year when I am very much dependent on the weather, hoping the rain holds off as much as possible before all the leaves have fallen. But of course this is a big ask and unrealistic as the leaves will continue to fall well into December!

The smoke tree by the picket fence has turned a fiery orange and red as the leaves are readying to drop. Bobette has once again started greeting me on the picket fence when I turn up for work in the mornings, and she stands right in front of the smoke tree, which creates an amazing backdrop for a photo session. The results are stunning.

Autumn is tightening its grip as the leaves start to fall en masse, and I spend much of my time keeping the lawns and paths clear. I leave some of the leaves on the flowerbeds for as long as possible and in areas of little importance as it's important for the wildlife, especially the birds. When the weather turns cold the leaves provide shelter for insects, and quite often I'll see the birds turning the leaves in search of a meal, especially blackbirds and robins who flick the leaves over with their beaks to see if there is anything underneath. In this garden, where the robins live, there is a good balance between well-kept and wildlife-friendly spaces, with plenty of wild areas, so I feel able to please both my customers *and* the wildlife.

Down by the lake, next to a clump of willow trees, is a bonfire site. At this time of year I will burn anything that is non-compostable, such as tree branches. One day I made my way down to the fire pit with more things to burn. To my surprise I was greeted by the sight of two small eyes among the branches of the bonfire! It was a little owl standing on the floor of the pit. I'd never seen one before, so it was a real treat! When it saw me the owl panicked and took flight, landing on a nearby hazel tree. I quietly followed and could just about see it. It was incredible. It amazes me, too, that I'm outside for most of my working day, yet there is so much of our wildlife that I rarely see.

It also served as a great reminder that you should move around what you intend to burn before setting it alight! I always pile the bonfire up and start a fire next to it, slowly feeding the fire with the material that needs burning. This not only allows any wildlife sheltering in the woodpile to escape but makes the fire much easier to control.

* * *

December brought with it the arrival of a new robin! It has forged its own territory between that of Bobette and Chip, taking control of the plum tree and so shrinking Bobette's territory. Bobette doesn't seem to be too unsettled. In fact she's surprisingly tolerant of it, just as Bob was with her and Bobbin when they first arrived on the scene. Maybe it is one of her offspring from earlier in the year. The new robin watched me interacting with Bobette, so I offered it a mealworm. Hesitantly, it built up the courage to fly to my hand and take it, and with that the ice was broken.

Whether I like it or not, this robin is now part of the family. I shared footage of it with my followers on social media and it immediately won hearts, with some comparing its boldness to Bob's: apt, considering that the plum tree was now its home. I invited my social media followers to name the newcomer and 'Lucky' was suggested a few times so that was what I settled on. I thought it fitting because the robin is lucky to live in such a robin-friendly garden and also because my followers and I are lucky to get to know it.

Lucky may well be one of Bobette's offspring, which could explain why she's so tolerant, but I can't be sure. The Christmas season arrived, and Joanna and I got to celebrate our wedding anniversary on 21 December, which just so happens to be 'National Robin Day'. What a coincidence!

* * *

In late December we entered a prolonged cold snap with temperatures barely exceeding 0°C during the day. I knew the robins would be struggling to find food with the ground being frozen solid and most insects hibernating to keep safe and warm. I did my best to visit them every day to ensure they had enough food to be able to survive the freezing nights.

When I arrived on 2 January, I saw Bobette flying across the drive in my direction as I was going through the gate and pulling into the drive – she must've seen me coming or she knew the sound of my car. She landed on the passenger-side wing mirror and looked at me through the window. Pip had also seen me pull up and was soon perched on the wing mirror on the other side. I opened my door, and Pip immediately flew into the car and landed on my right leg! He wanted some food of course, but the warmth of the space must've been welcome too. I gave him some suet pellets and mealworms, and he flew off. Then Bobette landed on my leg, before flying past me and settling on the passenger seat. And there she stayed contentedly, enjoying some suet pellets and mealworms. I could see that she was totally relaxed and very comfortable in her surroundings. This was particularly lovely because her only way out was to fly back past me! I didn't want to scare her, so I was very deliberate and calm with everything I did. Suffice to say we were comfortable in each other's company!

Bobette remained there for ten or fifteen minutes, happily warming her feet on the seat and eating the food. Then Pip returned and perched on my leg again. I could feel the cold from his feet through my trousers, so I was glad to provide him with some warmth. For territorial birds, they were both very civilized as they shared both the space and the food, with no fighting. It was a delightful experience, and I was pleased to be able to film them for my followers on social media too! I knew that they would have to get out of my car sooner or later, so I put down the passenger-side window using the button on the door and eventually they went their separate ways. Bobette certainly knew when the window was up or down – clever thing!

I then made my way to the compost bins where Chip lives and left a pile of mixed seed, peanuts, sunflower hearts, mealworms and suet pellets on a post for him and the other birds who would need a little extra boost. And I did see Chip tucking in. I then worked my way back to the mixed hedge – Lucky and Bobette occupy half each – leaving food on all the posts for them and the other birds, like the great tits and blue tits. I did see Lucky, and Bobette had followed me from the car to her half of the hedge at the end of her territory, so of course I left more food for her too, and also left piles under the yew hedge.

I will continue to do this for as long as I need to. When robins work their way into your heart they become very difficult to ignore, even when they're living in another town.

* * *

Meanwhile, Lucky has pushed right into Bobette's territory. I heard him singing in a tree near to the house, with Bobette's former partner nowhere to be seen. It would appear, then, that Lucky and Bobette have paired up and will potentially be a breeding pair come the spring. So this would seem to confirm that he is not her son! It is not uncommon for robins to start seeking partners during January, and I have seen this many times with other robins I've known. I have never been certain that robins pair up with the same partner year after year, and the fact that Bobette appears to have chosen Lucky as her potential suitor rather than her previous partner would appear to confirm it. But of course, it might work differently with every robin.

The next day it became apparent that Bobette and Lucky were indeed an item. They had taken complete control of the territory from the main house all the way down the length of the garden, past the plum tree to the end of the mixed hedge and the fence dividing the orchard from the garden, which borders Chip's territory. They were happily going around together and following me as I worked, but it was very clear that Bobette was the boss! It is still early days in the relationship. They are getting used to one another and there are boundaries, especially where Bobette is concerned.

Lucky does have a cheeky way about him. He isn't shy and will put himself wherever he wants to be, seemingly with little thought for the consequences! I do love all their individual characteristics. That day, I decided to have my coffee break with the robins, and sat on the step leading onto the lawn where I park the car, underneath the tree where Lucky had been singing the day before. As I sat there with my legs crossed out in front of me, it didn't take long for Bobette to join me. She happily hopped around beside me and then perched on my boot, and I offered her some suet pellets and mealworms.

Lucky, who was in the tree to my right and singing on a branch above us, then came to join us, making the mistake of landing on my other boot. I had my legs crossed so my boots were touching, and, with Bobette perched on the other one, he was far too close for her liking. He made a hasty retreat once Bobette gave him a stern telling-off – although she was silent, her beak was wide open and aimed in his direction. She was certainly letting him know who was boss!

In the next few days, I get the money shot. I'm sitting on the step, legs stretched out in front of me, coffee in one hand, Bobette and Lucky perched on each of my boots watching me, and my dogs, Pup and Saa, lying on the lawn in front of us minding their own business. You had to see it to believe it! Naturally, I did film the moment, and I shared it with my followers on social media. The post was viewed more than 1.4 million times on Instagram and received over 100,000 likes!

Although I have known Lucky for only a short period of time, he is very at ease in my presence. He is probably following Bobette's lead on this. I have never known both male and female to be so comfortable around me, especially the female. In the case of Bobbin and Ruby, Bobbin was very confident with me, but Ruby was far more reserved and unfortunately my relationship with them ended far too soon with the disappearance of Bobbin. These are very exciting times for me, and in being able to observe both male and female robins I am sure that I will learn many new things. And they're a breeding pair, too!

Both Pip and Chip have also paired up with new partners. I have seen both of them with another robin, which is great news! Pip does seem to have become a little more reserved and slightly less approachable, and now that Bobette and Lucky have become an item he is very reluctant to venture out of his territory. Maybe they are a very strong, dominant couple, and Pip is aware of it so is being cautious. But he is well, and that's the main thing. I still make sure to leave food for both him and Chip in order to make the winter days a little easier.

I will always miss Bob, and though I am very fond of the robins I share the garden with now, I will always cherish the relationship we had as a particularly special one. The time Bob and I spent together still impacts me today, and his legacy is still alive in the garden as I get to know the other robins, some of whom are possibly his offspring. It feels even more special that I am able to share this legacy with the rest of the world.

Through sharing photos of Bob and the garden, I hope that I am encouraging others to slow down a little, and take the time to notice the wildlife we share our spaces with. Reciprocating Bob's curiosity and interest in me resulted in an unlikely and beautiful friendship, but it also changed my ongoing relationship with the other creatures in the garden. I now notice the small things more often, and look out for ways I can support and encourage the wildlife around me. Bob has changed my life for the better, and I hope that he can do the same for others.

# Afterword

Life continues under the watchful eye of the old plum tree, where once upon a time a robin befriended me. Recently, as I made my way down the garden to the tree, I was greeted by the most welcome sight: both Bobette and Lucky perched there, Lucky on Bob's branch and Bobette on the branch behind him. For me, the plum tree is the heart of everything. It's where it all began with Bob, and it's been witness to so many wonderful moments that seeing them together in the plum tree was very special for me. Of course there are boundaries between the pair. They won't snuggle up side by side, or anything like that. But they are clearly together, while keeping a little distance. I am sure that they will make a fantastic partnership throughout the spring and breeding season, but when it's all over, they will separate and each will go their own way to survive the winter.

As I write this, January is coming to an end, and with that Bobette is becoming more tolerant of Lucky, allowing him to be in her space more. I have also become accustomed to spending my coffee breaks with the robins, often sitting on the step underneath the tree. I sit with my legs stretched out in front of me, and the robins always join me. Bobette will happily sit right next to me on the step while Lucky is more fidgety. He will come close, but he's always moving about. On a couple of occasions, though, they have both perched on my feet, one on each boot. Bobette and Lucky continue to provide an amazing insight into the world of a breeding pair, and they have won the hearts of all my followers on social media.

As the new year gets going, everything in the garden seems to be coming out of hibernation. Soon, in spring, I will see the daffodils coming into flower – always a spectacle as the grass islands surrounding the fruit trees in the orchard become a sea of yellow, bringing with them the optimism of new life. The sound and sight of geese as they fly overhead at dawn will become a more frequent occurrence – a nostalgic and always welcome scene. Already, there are buds on the apple trees, closed now, but readying themselves to burst into bloom. Spring is my favourite time of the year. With it comes the anticipation of warmer days and the vibrant colours that return to bring hope for the year ahead.

And of course, I look forward most of all to meeting the next generation of birds living under the old plum tree in the small town of Edenbridge.

# Acknowledgements

Thank you to my family for teaching me to value and care for the world around me and to love animals. Life wasn't always easy growing up, but I was surrounded by wildlife, the great outdoors, my family and of course my friends.

Thank you also to my dad, for instilling in me such a passion and love for history that I walk my hometown of Edenbridge not just in the present but also visualizing the past and the importance of remembering it. I also think of the future, hoping that maybe one day people will read my books and try to imagine Edenbridge and my world through my eyes. I hope it gives them the same sense of love and belonging that I feel when I walk the historic streets.

My friends have always been so important to me; they are my family too, and I thank them for sharing the highs and lows of my life with me as well as I theirs, always encouraging me to do the best and be the best I can.

Joanna, my wife, thank you for being the most amazing, supportive person in my life. I can safely say that I never would've written a book, switched on the computer or created anything Putman and Robin related if it wasn't for her.

Of course, to all my Putman and Robin followers, thank you for following my story and being a huge part of my life. I have shared photos and videos of the robins and other animals with you pretty much every day since 2015. We have shared the highs and the lows, the laughter and the tears. Thank you for being with me.

Thank you to my editor, Jessica, for encouraging

me to write this book and for guiding me every step of the way, as well as Rosie and all at Gaia and Octopus Publishing Group.

I am very much indebted to all the robins, Dave the crow, and the foxes for allowing me to view the world through their eyes and enabling me to record and share it with the world. Thank you, all of you.

# About the Author

Tony Putman is a gardener and passionate wildlife photographer who has captivated the world with his enchanting relationship with a Robin and a Fox. Developing a friendship with both that demonstrates beautifully the extraordinary capacity for a connection between wildlife and humans, he has been captured on film by the BBC in compelling footage that has drawn comments from admirers all over the world. His story and his work has catapulted Tony to the attention of BBC Springwatch, Fox News USA and Belgian, Dutch and German television channels.

# Praise for Tony Putman

'A heartwarming story of connection; this book will inspire you to see Nature with fresh eyes.'
*Suzy Reading*

'A beautiful and touching celebration of wildlife and our relationship with the little creatures who share this wonderful planet with us. This book is much needed in these chaotic times.'
*Abigail Hopkins*

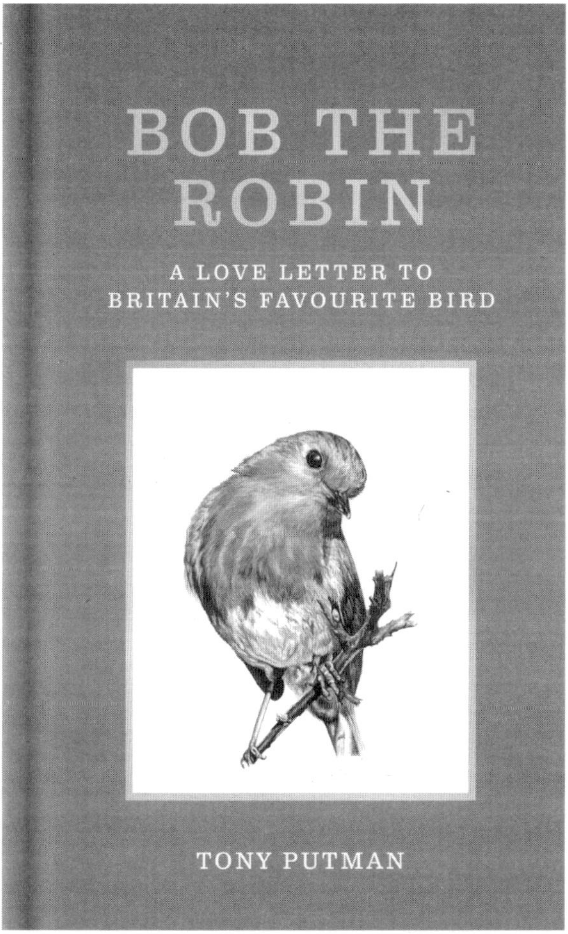


Also published by Gaia
ISBN 9781856755320

RAISING READERS

Books Build Bright Futures

Dear Reader,

We'd love your attention for one more page to tell you about the crisis in children's reading, and what we can all do.

Studies have shown that reading for fun is the **single biggest predictor of a child's future life chances** – more than family circumstance, parents' educational background or income. It improves academic results, mental health, wealth, communication skills, ambition and happiness.[1]

The number of children reading for fun is in rapid decline. Young people have a lot of competition for their time. In 2024, 1 in 10 children and young people in the UK aged 5 to 18 did not own a single book at home.[2]

Hachette works extensively with schools, libraries and literacy charities, but here are some ways we can all raise more readers:

- Reading to children for just 10 minutes a day makes a difference
- Don't give up if children aren't regular readers – there will be books for them!
- Visit bookshops and libraries to get recommendations
- Encourage them to listen to audiobooks
- Support school libraries
- Give books as gifts

There's a lot more information about how to encourage children to read on our website: **www.RaisingReaders.co.uk**

Thank you for reading.

hachette LIVRE

---

[1] OECD, '21st-Century Readers: Developing Literacy Skills in a Digital World', 2021, https://www.oecd.org/en/publications/21st-century-readers_a83d84cb-en.html

[2] National Literacy Trust, 'Book Ownership in 2024', November 2024. https://literacytrust.org.uk/research-services/research-reports/book-ownership-in-2024